Thanatos

Thanatos
Lilly's Project & The Void

Matthew Breuer

Publisher: Lulu.com

ISBN: 978-1-4357-4190-4

To order books by Matt, visit NewLifeFromHeaven.com

Thanatos
(θάνατος),
in Ancient Greek,
means death.

But this book
points the way
to life.

Dedicated
to the
LORD
God
of Abraham, Isaac, & Jacob;
The Only Begotten Son of God,
Jesus
Christ;
&
The
Holy
Spirit

Acknowledgments

I have deep appreciation for the following people for their contributions to Thanatos:

Thanks to Ann B., Paul B., and Sarah B. for reading the early manuscript of Lilly's Project.

Thanks to Martha K. for her thorough look at the framework of the whole book.

Thanks to Cassie P. for her comprehensive editing; any remaining mistakes are the author's errors.

Thanks to Patricia H. for her enthusiasm for and edits of Lilly's Project.

Thanks to Mike H. for his wise advice regarding changes to The Void.

Book 1
Lilly's Project

Book 2
The Void

Lilly's Project

Table of Contents

1~Joey

Lilly sat at her computer trying to figure out what to type. Her wacko algebra teacher had them writing papers about ancient mathematicians. Lilly thought that writing papers in English class was enough. She had started to drift off into a day dream, when her Mother came into the room.

~Lilly, it's bedtime.

~Yes, mother.

Lilly hated having to be told to go to bed, especially when she was trying to get her homework done. She reluctantly got under her butterfly covers and prayed a short prayer before being put to sleep by the sand man.

The sand storm was utterly destructive. Sandman was infuriated that Tooth Fairy was disturbing his victims. The contract stated that she had to keep the children from waking up during her work. Tooth Fairy failed and Sandman was going to get even. He tortured the children with nightmares beyond belief. Making them dream about death by burning, drowning, crucifixion, and impalement was only the beginning. Spiders, ghouls, demons, dragons, Dracula, imps, ogres, and all abominable creatures imaginable filled the dreams of the children.

Feeling miserable and guilty for the terror she caused, Tooth Fairy spent the night using sleeping powder to comfort all who needed her. A week from this Wednesday she was to appear before the Royal

Committee on Nighttime Affairs. Fearing the worst, she tried to score as many points as possible with the Governor. Buying the Governor presents, mixing sugar plums into his dreams, and loving the children should all make up for the rule she broke. A smiling Governor meant Tooth Fairy could relax a bit.

Ring. Ring. The alarm clock lurched Lilly from her dreams. Today was a grand day. A brilliant physicist was to give a lecture after school about the Origin of Space, Time, and Matter. Lilly leaped from her bed and put on a pink and white dress. She rushed downstairs and ate her oatmeal with fervor. Her bothersome mother reminded her to take her antibiotic. A stray dog had taken a chunk of skin from her ankle and the family feared an infection.

The bus pulled up in front of the house. Joey Richards, the bus driver, was a strange fellow. Sometimes he would be driving along and all of a sudden pull over on the roadside. The kids would all ask him what was wrong, but he never answered. Just as quickly as he pulled over, he would start driving again.

Parents had started calling the Bus Services Manager to voice their concern over Mr. Richards. The Manager reassured the parents that he was only going to give Joey another week to improve his behavior.

Lilly wondered if there was any way she could figure out what was wrong with Joey. She always sat up front on the bus and chatted with him. She enjoyed his company because he always seemed to care about her thoughts. He never belittled her or called her stupid. Other kids at school always tormented Lilly for looking funny. She wore oversized brown glasses and eccentric earrings, and she always asked too many questions in class. Most kids her age hated school.

Normally, Lilly enjoyed classes, but today she could not focus on what her teachers were saying. The physicist occupied her mind. What would he say? How could nothing produce everything? She was fascinated by the Big Bang theory, but she could not get over its basic flaws; it seemed too hard to accept. The theory stated that the universe always existed and continually recreated itself. On the other hand, her pastor told her God created the world a few thousand years ago. Lilly was not quite sure what to believe. She was always told most scientists believed in natural theories which explained all that was, is, and ever will be, but God had always been a huge part of her life. God was the only comfort she had when faced with the death of her grandpa.

Grandaddy had a fierce loyalty to God and His Word. This faith reassured Lilly that if she believed like her Grandaddy, she would see him again in Heaven.

The end of the school day was fast approaching. While marking off the minutes until class was over, Lilly began to contemplate the nature of time. If there were no matter moving through space there would be no time.... She thought that time was what kept everything from happening at once.... Knowing that the Physicist would explain everything, Lilly restrained her mind from stretching too far, too fast. Finally, the school day ended.

The auditorium was filled with a bunch of adults and older kids; Lilly felt out of place, but she did not let that distract her. A white haired man came out from behind the blue curtain and called everyone to attention. The crowd sat down and waited patiently for the scientist to begin. The man flashed complicated pictures up on the wall and used humongous words. Lilly had no idea what the man was saying. An hour and a half later, the man took a bow and walked off the stage to shake hands with the crowd. He was also selling his book and charging extra for a signature. Lilly heard some of the adults complain that the man talked a bunch of nonsense and had no idea how the universe began or will end. Lilly was glad to know that she was not the only one that was left in the dark.

Time kept marching on and before Lilly fully comprehended the reality of a decade, it had passed.

Graduation from college was the happiest day of Lilly's life. She had lined up a job at the National Center for Biological Studies. Her mission was to understand the human genome. Even though this was an extremely high goal, she maintained it anyway. Even if she reached for the stars and failed, she might land on the moon. Her three-year boyfriend James had encouraged her to pursue her scientific studies even though she wanted to dedicate her life to God. He convinced her that the spiritual life did not provide a substantial income and that science was where the money was. Lilly caved to James' influence.

~Lilly, what's going on?

James asked her with only an ounce of concern.

~I just read in the obituaries that Joey Richards died. He was my bus driver when I was in middle school. He was one of the few adults who understood me at that time. It's funny how they leave out the cause of death.

~Maybe it was too gruesome to say to the public.

Offering this tiny condolence, James was more concerned with who would win the hockey tournament than with a childhood memory. He thought it was ridiculous to be concerned about someone's death.

His reasoning was as follows: everyone was going to die sooner or later and it was best to accept this. He did not fear dying, for he had always been told by his parents that "once you're dead, you're dirt." The Christians were worried about hell, the Muslims were fanatical over sensual rewards in the afterlife, and most Eastern religions were concerned with escaping the endless cycle of reincarnation. James saw all of this as wasted energy. Happiness in this life was all he needed.

The weekend was over and Lilly started to get ready for work. She completed all her tasks at the house, which included fifteen minutes in the bathroom putting on make-up (even though James told her she was beautiful "in the natural" without all that "crap" on her face). Lilly awoke early every day to get to work before anybody else. She wanted to be the one to discover the genes that might lead to a cure for cancer.

Just as she was leaving the driveway, she heard a loud bark. She looked into her rear-view mirror and saw a mangy mutt sitting behind the car. She paused. Lilly was afraid to get out, as she had had an unpleasant interaction with a dog when she was younger. Sitting there for a minute in park, she decided she would back up slowly and hope the dog would just leave. She put the car in reverse and looked in the mirror before backing out any farther, but the dog had already vanished. It struck her as odd how the mutt would just disappear.

The rest of the ride to work was uneventful, but Lilly could not keep her mind off of Joey. She remembered how he taught her how to kiss. One morning, Joey had brought two balloons on the bus. He had drawn funny faces on them and chuckled at the thought of his lesson. When Lilly got on the bus, he handed her a balloon. Lilly was puzzled, but giggled when Joey started to kiss his balloon. She would never forget that day.

Lilly arrived at the lab, turned on the lights, made a pot of coffee, and started running tests. When her colleagues began to arrive, Lilly decided to take a break. She went to the lounge and grabbed a newspaper. Being a news-junkie was in her nature; she wanted to be a know-it-all. The police beat was always intriguing. Today, there was a report on a homeless drunk that killed a man. In the last few sentences it revealed that the murdered man was Joey Richards. Lilly dropped the paper to the floor and started to cry. Lilly did not understand how this news would bring up tears. A co-worker came in to get some coffee and saw Lilly. The coworker was one to mind his own business and did not even ask what was wrong. Lilly decided to take the rest of the day off. She had already put in enough extra hours that it did not make a difference to her boss whether she did this every now and then.

She drove home in a dulled state, trying to remember everything she could about Joey. Lilly remembered that the parents of the children on her bus route succeeded in getting Joey fired from the bus route. Afterwards, Joey started to appear in the newspaper as a late blooming, body builder. The last award he received was just in the paper two months ago, so she knew he was still buff. How could a homeless man who was probably weak from hunger and intoxicated with booze murder a formidable man like Joey? She smelled more trouble than what appeared on the surface. Deciding to take her vacation early and stay at home instead of going to Florida, she spent some time walking around town talking to homeless people. There were more than she would have thought. She hoped that nobody would ask for money, because she didn't have any on her and didn't want to appear cold-hearted. A middle-aged lady was one of the first street persons Lilly encountered. Unsure of how to approach a complete stranger and talk about a murder, Lilly began simply.

~Hello.

Lilly spoke cautiously as she approached a well-weathered woman.

~How long have you been homeless?

~I have been on the streets for two years, ever since my husband left me for another woman and stole all our money. So much for what's mine is yours.

~How did your husband get all the money?

~He was a lawyer and knew all the forms to sign in order to transfer all our finances and assets into his sole possession.

Lilly gave a brief thought to James. She wondered if she better find out about these papers before him.

~My name is Lilly. Would you be willing to tell me your name?

~Sure, Lilly. Most people call me Anna. I call myself that too.

Anna chuckled quietly.

~Anna, have you heard anything about a murder around here?

~There are a bunch of men that live over on Third Street in the empty shoe factory. Sometimes these fellows get into trouble. I am not sure if one could be a murderer, but it is possible. I would be careful about going over there. I have an extra bottle of pepper spray if you would like it.

~Thank you, Anna. I'll take the pepper spray and give it back to you on my way out.

Lilly walked over to the shoe factory on Third with purpose in her step. Determined to get to the bottom of this mess, she was ready to risk going into a run-down building filled with sketchy men.

She arrived at the employee entrance. Slowly, but confidently, she stepped through the portal. A flashlight would have been helpful. Going a little farther in, her eyes began to adjust and the stray rays of light coming through some of the windows that were not boarded up helped her to see. Out of nowhere a hand clasped over her mouth. She screamed, but no sound was heard. Terrible thoughts of losing her life flashed before her mind. The voice from the figure was trying to calm her down, but she kept fighting to get free. Her courage slithered out of her. Next thing she knew, a dim lantern was turned on. Another man was telling Bob to get his hands off the lady because he didn't want to give the police any more reason to arrest them. Bob cussed at Mac and finally let go. Lilly's heart was trying to slow, her head to clear, and her lungs to breathe.

~What is your name, Miss?

~Lilly.

Lilly remembered she had the spray and was debating whether or not to use it. She wondered if these men knew anything about the murder of Joey, but they also might murder her. Realizing that she would have a hard time getting them both in the eyes at the same time, Lilly restrained her fear and let some of her scientific, analytic mind take control. She asked them for a minute to regain her composure. Lilly knew that the easiest way to get a man talking was to turn on the sex appeal. She pulled out a mirror and reapplied lipstick. Mac and Bob both gazed at her. Lilly knew she could get them talking.

~Why are you guys hiding from the police?

Bob decided to respond.

~Mac and I robbed a gas station a few days ago. Our boss, Zhang Chi, told us we had to cause some trouble that night.

~I don't follow you, Bob.

16

Lilly tried to sound brave and curious. She also feigned a smile.

Mac, the more intelligent of the two, responded.

~Mr. Chi told us that a murder was to take place that afternoon and he needed the cops to be out and about so as to keep them away from the scene.

Remembering that the notice of death was in the paper on Saturday and that the news of the murder was Monday, she made a mental time line. Knowing that dates and times and every little bitty detail was important, she knew she would have to start a notebook. She wondered if she was a little crazy for becoming so involved in the matter and not giving the police any chance. It had only been a few days.

~Do you know where the scene was? And do you know what the murder was all about?

Lilly was trying to gather her thoughts.

Mac replied.

~Ma'am. Mr. Chi performs a few murders a month and he usually never tells us any details. I can give you his business phone number if you would like.

~What type of business?

~He's a mortician. You know, a dead beat for the dead.

~Good one, Mac.

Bob hollered in his dim-witted way.

~Here is Mr. Chi's card. He is always trying to get business in killing and cremating.

Further freaked out by the guys, Lilly decided they did not know enough about the murder. Her best bet was to try to figure out more about Mr. Chi. She took the business card, offered her thanks, and stepped back into the light.

2~Dinner

Lilly arrived home to find her boyfriend James drinking a lemon flavored beer.

~Where have you been, Lilly?

~I was just walking around town getting my exercise.

He didn't need to know all her secrets. And she had plenty.

~I was wondering if you wanted to go out to dinner. Lilly, we seem to be growing apart. Not much, but I just feel we are not as close as we used to be. Do I have an accurate hunch about this?

~I think a romantic dinner might be a wonderful idea.

James jumped up from the couch and brushed a few chip crumbs off his shirt. Lilly had gotten used to his constant snacking. Being fat was out of the question. Lilly made James go out on Sunday evening walks. Long walks. Seeing him huff and puff a little gave her a sense of satisfaction. The two of them headed over to the garage and Lilly set the house alarm system. James took the driver's seat and left Lilly shotgun. The drive over to Dos Gringos was punctuated with conversation and then silence. A Mexican quartet was out front singing and waiters were visible serving people outside. The evening was slightly breezy and warm.

~James, let's sit outside.

~I would prefer the air conditioning.

James had an authoritative tone in his voice. Lilly was unsure of the reason for his superior attitude.

~Okay. As long as we can sit away from the bar. I want to stay cancer free.

James still didn't agree.

~I'm going to smoke. We're going to sit at the bar for awhile.

Lilly pondered his attitude. The bartender was overly friendly with Lilly and Lilly let him know it.

~Sir! Stop flirting with me! I have a boyfriend!

Lilly could take it no longer and asked James to finish his cigar. James puffed once more, threw the remains in an ash tray, and gave Lilly directions.

~Let's go take a seat over by the taco buffet. I could eat at least ten tonight.

~James, you always exaggerate. Last time you only had five and a half.

~Lilly, why do you always have to correct me?

~I like to be accurate.

~Fine. But you don't have to force everybody else around you to be perfect.

The rest of the meal was eaten in silence. Finally, James burped and got up to leave. Lilly followed. The owner offered his farewell.

~Thank you for coming to Dos Gringos! We hope to see you again soon!

The ride home was awkward. Lilly tried multiple times to discuss topics of neutral emotion. Even sports could not get a response. As they were turning on to their street, they saw two cops in their driveway.

~What the hell?

James exclaimed.

They drove to the curb of their house and were shocked to see a man being thrown into the back of the cop car. Lilly was jolted out of her thoughts and opened the car door and stepped out. A police woman asked her if she was the owner of the property.

~Yes. James and I. Umm. I am Lilly Summer and this is James Clark.

~Hello, Ma'am. So what happened to our house?

James seemed to lift his spunky anger from Lilly and redirect it to the perpetrator of the trespassing.

~Your security alarm went off and we drove right over to see a man inside your house looking through your computer. We had the feeling that this was not a resident that accidentally set off their own alarm, so we stormed the house. It was a wise move on your part to have the break in alarm set to silent for fifteen minutes so that we could get over here before the perp knew he was in a pickle. Home owners that set their burglar alarm to sound immediately rarely end up getting any of their stuff back and we seldom catch the law breaker. The criminal knows that they have a few minutes to collect before the cops get there. The alarm just gives them a time frame.

~Thank you for catching the crook.

Lilly said appreciatively.

~Thanks.

James added as an afterthought.

~We're going to take him down to the slammer to question him on his motives. Most criminals go for money. This guy was going for information. We found no valuables on him; he was just snooping through your computer files. You don't have to answer this question, but it might be helpful for the investigation. What type of information do you have on that hard drive anyway?

~Some computer games.

James responded dumbly.

~I have data from biological tests that I performed at work.

~And what are you experimenting on?

~I am working on a cure for cancer.

~Interesting.

The officer replied approvingly.

~I wonder why he would not go to your work place?

~Well, to be honest with you officer, I keep all my important files at home. I do not want any of the other scientists to nose around in my files and take credit for my work. We work as a team on some projects, but this cancer issue is all my own. Have you heard the story of Rosalind Franklin?

~Sorry, Miss Lilly, I can't say I have.

~You should check up on that sometime. Her story is quite a motivation for women.

~I'll do that, but right now my partner and I have to get back to the station. We'll give you a full report in a few days. You might get a call from the captain to ask you a few questions. This was not a normal burglary.

~Wait! Before you leave, can you tell me anything about the murder of Joey Richards?

~I can't, sorry. But my partner can. Rick was at the scene.

~Rick, get over here! I'll go back to the car to keep an eye on things. Bye Mr. Clark, Miss Summer.

~How can I help you?

~Do you have any idea if Joey Richards was killed on purpose or by accident?

~I can tell you it was no accident. He was brutally tortured. The guy was shot 7 times, one of his hands and one of his feet were cut off, three of his fingers on the other hand were missing, and the worst part was how they cut open his belly in an x fashion and strung out his intestines all over the place. They also stuffed chunks of fool's gold down his throat. The murderer is a freakin' freak if you ask me. Murders like this imply that the killer was trying to give somebody a message. Usually, only the receiver of that message understands. It's beyond me. Is there anything else you want to know?

~I think I've heard enough!

Vomit was beginning to crawl up Lilly's throat. Tears began flowing down her cheeks and then vomit projected on to the front lawn. James stepped back, out of the way, while Rick tried to comfort her. Rick, trying to distract Lilly, continued talking.

~We took plenty of pictures of the interior so you could compare it to what you knew you had. This is just in case the thief actually took something. If you find anything missing, let us know. But like my partner said, we found nothing on him. We have to get him to the station. Bye.

James guided a weeping Lilly into the house. Bed was the only matter important to Lilly; sleep could wipe away all the horrible images. James walked her to the bedroom and tucked the covers around her. He tried to console her and convince her that she was safe, but she knew otherwise.

~Darn it, James! You know the house was just broken into. Somebody must want something from us!

~I have no idea what's going on, Lilly. Try to get some sleep. You still have a few more days off from work. Try to make the best of that time. Maybe you should have gone to Florida. Sunshine, beaches, hot guys...

~Stop, James. You're not helping me feel better. Good night.

Turning off the lamp on her bedside, Lilly closed her eyes and pretended to fall asleep. After a few minutes of sitting on the side of the bed, James crept out of the room. He went to watch the late hour comedy show. A laugh would be good medicine for this upsetting situation. Lilly lay there staring at the ceiling. Thoughts stampeded through her mind. What the heck is wrong with this world? What is it that makes humans so horrible and wicked? A voice in her mind recalled a Sunday school lesson that she had had many years ago. "Sin is the fatal problem of mankind, little Lilly. Sin causes man to hurt himself, others, and ultimately God. Sin is the reason God seems distant."

God had been distant from Lilly's mind for quite some time it seemed. She had let Him fade into the background of her life. This was the last thought she had before she fell asleep.

3~Boss

During the middle of the night, James was thrust awake by a blood-chilling scream.

~Lilly, it's not real. You're just having a nightmare.

~James, I know what's real. This place is real.

~What do you mean this place? Our house is real, you are real, I am real.

~There is a reality greater than all of this. You know what I am talking about James.

~Go back to bed before you hurt yourself, Lilly.

~I will not be silenced. I will tell my story. The STORY must be told.

***

Lilly finally dozed off again, but the rest of the night was filled with tossing and turning.

***

As usual, the darkness slowly gave rise to the light and the birds started chirping joyfully to nobody in particular.

Their song gently woke Lilly from her fitful slumber. Lilly thought the music of the birds was a wonderful gift. A thought not yet recognizable drifted into Lilly's consciousness. Blinking her eyes and stretching her arms, Lilly realized she never gave Anna back her pepper spray. A force not all her own lifted Lilly from bed and propelled her to put on gray sweat pants and a grey hoodie with a light running jacket over the top. Sleeping haphazardly on the couch was an overworked James. Overworked. Ha. That was funny.

He made big bucks for them in the stock market, but still, who was she kidding. As long as he knew when to buy and sell, all was fine, but if the stock market crashed, he would have to get a real job. Lilly considered mining or farming or working in a factory more of a real job than playing number games. Heck, it would be wonderful if he was a chemist.

Jogging would be the best way to get to the plot of unused land that Anna called her own. Nobody was out and about this early in the morning. Lazy-loafers.

Out of breath and exhausted, Lilly arrived at the plot. Going over to the pile of old newspapers that Anna covered herself in, Lilly could see Anna was sleeping. She would feel horrible waking her up, so she would just put the pepper spray next to her. Lilly had an odd feeling of a dark presence as she gingerly walked closer. Wondering if Anna was alright, Lilly leaned down towards her face to see if she was breathing. Her mouth was closed, her nostrils didn't flare, and her chest was stiff as a board. God help me! Lilly shook Anna with such gusto that any living person would wake up. To no avail. Anna was cold and must have been dead for a few hours.

Lilly wondered what any sane person would do if they found a dead body. She had no clue. Reaching into her left coat pocket, Lilly pulled out a card. It was Mr. Chi's Mortuary. Her racing mind jumped at the thought of having a valid reason for calling Mr. Chi. At least Anna's death would help provide a key to figuring out how Mr. Chi was connected to Joey. Mac said Mr. Chi was the one who arranged the murder, but then why would a homeless drunk be arrested? Did Mr. Chi set up the drunk to take the fall for the murder he performed? Lilly couldn't believe anyone would inflict such intricate and cruel mutilation upon a body. Lilly knew in her heart that Mr. Chi was the killer and the drunk was a decoy. A crucial idea was trying to surface in her mind, but was blocked out by her emotional state. She walked over to a bench and sat down to organize her thoughts. Number one: there was a dead body here. Number two: Joey Richards was dead. Number three: Mr. Chi was most likely involved in the murder of Joey. Number four: The dead body of Anna would give her a reason to call Mr. Chi. Bingo.

Out of her right pocket Lilly pulled a cell phone. 555-465-3454. Ring. Ring. Finally a low, grumpy voice answered.

~This is Zhang Chi. How may I help you? Or rather, who can I help you with?

~Hello, Mr. Chi. This is Lilly Summer and I am looking to take care of the dead body of a friend of mine. We are on 145 Second Street. I have no way to transport the body and I have no idea what to do. Can you help me?

~Calm down, Miss Summer! I handle dead bodies all the time. I can drive the hearse over there and help you deal with the body. I'll be over in a few minutes.

Click.

Lilly sat on the bench in silence. Hunger pangs began to rumble through her body. One piece of toast in the morning was not enough. Remembering she packed a granola bar in her coat pocket, she found the prize, unwrapped the bar, and began to fill her tummy.

A dreadful hearse pulled over to the side of the road. Having no idea what to expect, Lilly was surprised to see a gray-haired man with a tacky sweater step out of the car. His body looked buff and young, but his face gave the impression of a senior citizen. The man walked over to Lilly and grimly asked where the body was.

~Do you see the pile of newspapers over there in that corner?

~Yes.

~She is right over there.

Mr. Chi strolled over to the pile, removed all of the newspapers, lifted up the body, and carried her over and put her into the back of the hearse. Mr. Chi told Lilly to get in the car because he had some questions he had to ask. Lilly walked feebly over to the hearse, opened the passenger door, and sat down. Mr. Chi took the driver's seat and began question number one.

~How is that biological research on cancer going?

Lilly had no idea how he knew this much about her and why he would be asking.

~I think we have the more important matter of a dead body on our hands.

~Lilly Summer. I am in charge of this operation.

Mr. Chi locked the car in a flash, pulled out a gun from under his seat, and pointed it at Lilly before she had any idea what was going on. Telling her to shut up, he reached down again to find a role of duct

27

tape. Zhang roughly surrounded Lilly's mouth and wrists with tape.

~Listen here, woman. You will do as I say. Understand?

Lilly weakly nodded her head yes. Mr. Chi reached over the console and found a towel in the back seat. All of the sudden, he began to wipe off his face. The towel became filled with cheap, white make-up, and the wrinkles and pale color disappeared from Zhang's face. A chocolate brown tan was revealed and accented by the smooth skin of a young man. Startled, Lilly was dumb-founded by this disguise tactic. What was this man hiding?

Driving over to his funeral home, Mr. Chi let Lilly in on a few secrets. Admitting that he was the one that arranged the murder of Joey was only the beginning. The drunk was set up as a decoy and the deal worked out because prisoners are treated better than the homeless. The guy gets a secure room, with a toilet and sink, he gets to work out and read, and most importantly the man gets a tray full of food three times a day. This particular drunk did not care if he had to spend the rest of his life in jail; he was already sixty-six, depressed, and dulled by booze and drugs. Compared to this, the slammer sounded like a nice retirement. Lilly hadn't realized how horrible being homeless was compared to being incarcerated. Mr. Chi started to talk about the weather and sports and other such nonsense and Lilly's mind turned away from such trivialities.

Anna. That was all Lilly could think about. Why did I never take the time to get to know all these people out on the streets? Only when someone from my childhood got murdered and I could use these homeless people to my own advantage did I take any notice of their dignity and individuality.

Wondering if Lilly could figure out how to reach the ex-husband, she tried to think if she knew Anna's last name. She did not remember Anna telling her that bit of essential information. I must have been really uncaring when I talked to her. Self-centered.

Abruptly struck out of her thoughts, Lilly realized that her life was in danger. What type of danger this was she was not exactly sure. Does Mr. Chi want information, or revenge, or does he have some twisted sensual appetite? Will he kill me? What am I worth to him? Lilly tuned back into the babble of Zhang.

~Do you like this radio station, Lilly? I asked you a question!

Lilly tried to mumble a response. Mr. Chi realized that he still had the duct tape on her mouth. The habit of putting duct tape on his victims stemmed from the need to keep them from screaming or prevent them from asking too many stupid questions. The questions always annoyed Zhang. You're being kidnapped, deal with it. Reasoning that Lilly was intelligent enough to be calm without duct tape, Zhang leaned over and ripped it from Lilly's face. Zhang performed this with such force that Lilly began to bleed where the duct tape had just been secured to her face.

~Bastard!

~If that is all the bleeding you're going to have to deal with, you'll be lucky.

Lilly glared at Mr. Chi and Mr. Chi just focused on driving. Zhang became impatient and began his usual series of questions.

~So, what type of thoughts are going through your mind?

~I'd rather not say.

~Miss Summer, I think it would be in your best interest to tell me everything you know. And I mean everything.

~Where should I begin?

~Well, my history with you goes back a ways. Your friend Joey would talk about you sometimes. He would tell me about your love of science and concern for helping humanity. All that mush. I was friends with Joey also, before he became a weakling. Did you know that Joey was into drugs?

~You're lying! Joey was one of the most physically fit people I knew. The papers always featured articles about his athletic achievements. He steered clear of junk food, exercised continuously, and centered his life on healthy living. He just won an award for weight training a few months ago.

~You've been seriously deceived.

~How?

~Joey bought steroids from me on a regular basis.

~But the competitions he entered screen for steroid use.

~In the drug world, we know how to get around screenings. I will not reveal all my ways to you, but I will tell you that we have harmless looking drugs that cloak steroids. I also specialize in exotic drugs that are not tested for in a regular drug panel. Ha! Outsmarted you there, biologist.

~My area of expertise concerns DNA molecules and not chemical interactions induced by medication.

~There is something more you are not telling me, Miss Summer!

~What?

~What have you recently discovered concerning mitochondrial DNA, Glycerol-3-phosphate dehydrogenase, and gene splicing and recombination?

~I can't tell you that!

~Like I said before, you will tell me everything, even if it involves cutting off your fingers one by one; then I move on to your toes. I will progress until all nonessential appendages are cut off and I am the one who will determine which body parts I need functioning.

~You're an evil man!

~You know nothing, honey. There are more connections between Joey and I than you could imagine. They would make your head spin, but we will go into that later. Ah, we have just arrived at my cozy little funeral home.

The garage in the back was the perfect way to sneak bodies in and out of the morgue without anybody being the wiser.

The hearse pulled in and the garage door shut behind them. Lilly wondered if she would be able to escape. Zhang opened his door, squeezed around the car, and opened the door for Lilly like a true gentlemen. Lilly knew from experience that this man was rough, tough, and all business. No time would be wasted on any other manners of etiquette. This was only a mockery and joke in which Lilly was the butt end. Mr. Chi grinned at Lilly's disgust at him.

~You can either step out of the car on your own or I can force you out. Your choice.

Lilly chose the more pleasant manner.

~Right this way, Ma'am.

More of the fake pleasantries.

~I'm going to keep your wrists tied for now. I will assume that you are happy being restrained.

~I am not a docile woman, Mr. Chi.

~And neither am I. Take this seat right here!

Lilly sat with the resignation of a four year old being told to go to the corner for a timeout. Mr. Chi cracked a smile.

~I am sure you had an encounter with the man I sent to your house, but I bet you didn't realize he accomplished his mission.

~What are you talking about? The police caught him.

~Have you so quickly forgotten about my humanitarian activities?

~Oh, yeah. That's right. You use the misfortune of others to make your fortune. So that man received a nice cell too?

~Yes, Ma'am. But this guy will be getting a shorter sentence. After all, he only trespassed and nosed around on your computer. He didn't actually steal anything. At least not that the cops know about. This guy is also useful enough to me that I will be in touch with some bribed judges and lawyers.

~You twisted piece of crap.

Zhang slapped Lilly with the ferociousness of a caged tiger. With her hands coupled together, Lilly held her cheek as best as she could. All Lilly could do now was play along and find out where the maze led. She asked the obvious question.

~What was the mission that your man accomplished?

Zhang replied with a twisted smile.

~Does Project Thanatos sound familiar to you?

Lilly responded simply.

~Yes.

~I thought so.

~Well, I bet you're wondering how I found out about your little secret.

~I'm sure you would be thrilled to tell me.

Lilly said this with fake enthusiasm.

~How did you guess? I have a colleague that works in your lab as a janitor. Sometimes he likes to go through the trash to see what you brainiac scientists are working on. He came across some interesting information. Your achievements would become famous and you wanted to have a quick way to describe your success. So you wrote a summary of all you had accomplished. It's too bad you threw out your rough draft without shredding it. I guess even the brilliant make mistakes.

Just then Bob and Mac strolled in through the back door.

~Hey boss, how is it going? I see you have company.

Mac stated aloud; he looked delighted at the sight of an attractive female. The last time he saw her was in the dark. A cheap lantern does not cast that much light.

~Hot diggity dogs. We have a smokin' one here.

~Shut up, Mac! Can't you see I am having a chat with my dear Lilly?

~What are you talking about?

Mac asked with genuine interest.

~Well, maybe Lilly would be kind enough to explain to you what she has discovered.

Zhang spoke with wit.

31

~Do share, baby.

Mac said with a grin.

Lilly hated when brute men talked to her like she was a doll to be looked at and played with. What an insult to her intelligence. If only she could send these men to an obedience school.

Zhang began an elaborate speech.

~Lilly, I think it might be beneficial for all of us to have a first hand account of what you have managed to manipulate in the lab. Your short note just doesn't do you justice. And I had a hard time interpreting the data my subordinate stole from your computer and sent to me through e-mail. Although, the stolen data can be used to prevent you from turning to the cops. You wouldn't want me to give this data to another scientist, now would you? Then they would get all the fame and glory.

Hating the way they manipulated her, Lilly still wanted to keep these dangerous men happy. Who knew what they could do if you upset them?

~Well. Umm. My interest in science started at a young age, progressed through my college career by means of a major in Genetics and Cellular Biology, and culminated in my Project Thanatos.

~What the heck does that mean?

Bob looked extremely confused. That seemed to be a natural state for him.

~I discovered the very genes that determine when someone dies. I have secretly been working on a way to eliminate or rearrange those genes to prevent death altogether. I have a handful of mice in which I have spliced out the death gene thus causing their bodies to theoretically live forever. I am able to deliver a virus via a pill that injects my DNA modifier into every cell in the body within a few hours. The DNA change even allows the body to heal from fire burns, HIV, or other diseases. My next step is to test this on an elderly patient who is expected to die soon. If the signs of aging and death depart, I would know that I have made an achievement in line with those of Newton, Einstein, and Edison.

~Pretty impressive, right boys?

~Yes, Sir. Mr. Chi.

~Now, Lilly, I have some explaining to do.

~That would be appreciated.

Lilly said with sincerity.

Zhang began another lecture.

~Ever since my janitor friend found your little paper in the trash, I have become interested in this elixir of life. Who knows where the potential for these methods ends? We all have a desire to live forever. As Hamlet put it best, "But that the dread of something after death, The undiscover'd country from whose bourn, No traveller returns, puzzles the will, And makes us rather bear those ills we have, Than fly to others that we know not of?" You probably didn't think I knew literature, did you Miss Summer?

~You seem to be a cunning man to me; I will admit I seldom hear people quote Shakespeare.

Lilly vocalized her surprise.

~Well, to continue my story. I myself would love to taste of this magic and I have plenty of clients who would pay me huge sums of money to collect on this gift. That is where you come in, Miss Summer. I am going to steal your research and take credit for the whole shebang. Ha! I love evil.

~I won't let you do this!

~What type of position are you in to reason with me? Anyway, I stole all the information about your studies from your hard drive.

Lilly tried to counter his logic.

~Let me put it this way, Mr. Chi. Do you have the skills in genetic engineering that would allow you to master this discovery and interpret all that data?

~Well, I have thought about that end of the deal and that is the only, I repeat the only reason I am going to let you live. If I knew how to handle this all on my own, I would not have to worry about the possibility of you turning me in to the cops. As long as you're alive, you're a liability. In other words, you're right. I do need you. This is how it is going to work. You are going to take permanent leave from your job and work solely for me. You are going to tell all your relations that you have a job that you cannot resist. And that the catch of the job is that you can not tell them where it is or what it is about. Do you understand me?

~I still don't see how you are going to pull this off.

Lilly said this with a quiver in her voice.

Zhang projected a confident statement.

~Let me explain in more simple terms. I am going to place a tracking device on your ankle that is equipped with a microphone and shocking mechanism. If you start to say something or go somewhere that I would prefer you stay away from, I will send jolts of electricity through your body. Don't think that I have forgotten that you can write out that you need help, so I am going to have constant man surveillance upon you. I have two guys who are going to follow you most anywhere. I will give you the privacy of using the bathroom alone. You will tell anyone who asks that these men are from Scientific American and are looking to write a story on you. The men are Bob and Mac. You should become even more well acquainted. The only reason I'm going to let you out of here is so that you can gather all your supplies and set up your lab in the funeral home basement. You will also have just enough time to tell James that you hate him and never want to see him again. If you do not do this, you will end up like Joey and I will have to find another way to use your research. Did that all sink in?

~It seems that I really have no choice in the matter. I guess you're my new boss.

4~Data

The clock was nearing 3 PM, and James was becoming extremely worried about his girlfriend. He had already called Lilly's friends and family and was ready to call the police to file a missing person report. Unexpectedly, someone knocked at the front door. James answered; it was the guy cop from before.

~Hello, Mr. Clark

~It's Rick, right?

~Rick Pritchard to be exact.

~Mr. Pritchard, I need your help.

~Mr. Clark, I also need your help.

~You go first, Rick.

~I thought it necessary to tell you that we got your trespasser to confess, by means I would rather not tell, that he stole information from your computer. Your girlfriend told my partner that it was biological data. Why would a total stranger know about this data and why would they want it?

~You know, Lilly never tells me much about her work. I wonder if there is still a copy of the data on our computer. Let's go check.

The odd couple walked over to the PC and James started the computer up.

~Rick, did you watch the hockey game last night?

~No.

~Oh, well it was amazing. You should really get into the game.

~I have more important matters on my mind, solving crimes for instance.

~Yeah, I guess you're right. That kind of makes me feel unimportant. And then for a living, I steal money from ignorant people.

~Do I need to arrest you?

~No. I work on trading stocks, but I have inside help. This allows me to make big bucks off the little people who don't know what they're doing in the stock market.

~You slime bag. I'm all about helping the average man keep his money away from the scum on the streets.

~Sometimes, I feel like scum. For the past few weeks, my conscience has been bugging me. I really need moral help.

~James, you might as well get it off your chest.

~Lilly doesn't know that I mooch off my parents. They send money into my account every now and then. I tell my dad that I use it to play around in the stock market. Most of the time I double the money and give him back the original plus a few hundred bucks. I keep the rest that he doesn't know that I made. Then he gets the itching and sends me a few thousand again. He's a gambling addict and got his fortune from a mega lottery that he won ten years ago. He retired from his job and spends more time than ever in the casinos to the neglect of his wife. Even with all that money, he still wants to make more. I guess the love of money really is the root of all evil and I have inherited that love from my dad. Lilly thinks I know numbers well, but my tactics for making money include just a few tricks. I feel horrible about my life style sometimes. Especially when I treat Lilly the way I have been lately.

~You should go talk to a priest.

~I don't participate in religious rituals.

~Just a suggestion. Well, the computer is on the login screen.

~Umm. I guess I don't know the password to Lilly's account.

~Well, you're in luck that ranger Rick is here. I spent a year in college in a computer course. The prof spent more time teaching hacking then he did coding languages. Lucky for us. Give me a minute to try a few techniques and I'm sure I can get in. I mean, how hard can it be if our crook hacked in?

Rick clicked and typed faster than James had ever seen anyone do. Casually pulling out a USB port from his pocket, Rick plugged it in and brought up a hacking program. In a few seconds, the charming sound of windows logging in was heard.

Rick remained in control of the computer with James looking over his shoulder. James hated feeling inferior to other men. The superior need must be right from the y chromosome. Thinking about how watching sports was nothing compared to playing sports, James made up his mind to go to the gym as soon as he figured out what happened to Lilly. Feeling horrible for not bringing it up sooner, James blurted out.

~Rick! I have no idea where Lilly is. Can you help? She left early this morning without leaving a note. She is all about keeping me informed where she is and lately she has been acting weird. It must be something about Joey Richards, but she says I am too insensitive to notice. She takes my lack of talking for lack of caring.

~Hold on a minute! Maybe if we find out what type of data Lilly has on here, we can figure out where she is. Give me a couple of minutes to look over the most recent files.

James kept his further thoughts to himself.

~Here's a folder named Press Release of Project Thanatos. Maybe she was going to release news that someone would rather have her keep quiet. Let's look inside the folder. Empty. Damn.

Rick was extremely frustrated that the contents were gone.

~James, how about we get in my car and drive over to Lilly's lab?

~If you think that will help us find Lilly, let's go.

The two men strode out of the house and jumped into the cop car. Rick drove through the neighborhood onto the highway. Once on the highway, James was surprised that Rick turned on the siren, and alarmed that he was going well over the speed limit. The privileges of being a cop. Luckily, there was a parking spot on the street right out in front of the lab. James beat Rick out of the car, and climbed the stairs. James turned to see where Rick was, and noticed that he was on the car radio. Stopping to listen, James heard Rick file a missing person report with the station. Finishing up, Rick joined James.

The reception area was cluttered with scientific journals and potted plants, making the room seem quite small. James was embarrassed that he didn't even know where Lilly's office was. A man in a white coat was about to walk by when James interrupted the man on his mission.

~Excuse me, Sir. Could you point me to Lilly Summer's office.

~Who are you, exactly?

~I'm Lilly's boyfriend. I'm trying to find her.

~Well, her office is on the third floor, room number 312.

~Thanks. Catch you later.

~Sure.

The two men found the elevator, pressed the third floor button, and waited to be free from the boring, corny elevator music. Reaching Lilly's office was like trying to find cheese in a maze. James could have sworn the room numbers were in no ordering system known to man.

Finally, Lilly's office was discovered. James reached for the door knob and realized it was locked.

~Now what do we do?

~Calm down, James. We're in luck. My sergeant advised me to carry a lock picking kit in my belt. Let me see if I can break in. Just act like we know what we are doing.

Click!

The locking mechanism was satisfied that it had been unlocked and thus popped open. If only women were as easy to crack open. James usually had a hard time understanding all the clues that Lilly left for him. How was he supposed to know that a toothpaste cap had to be put back on or that the toilet seat had to be left down or that black pants and a dark blue shirt do not go together? He was never even sure if the dress matching was right. Maybe black and blue do go together; James truly didn't care, but he still tried to do what was necessary to please Lilly.

Rick sat down in Lilly's chair and began the ritual of unlocking the computer. Lilly tied up her work tighter than Fort Knox. Deciding that he should make himself useful, James started going through the paperwork on Lilly's desk. Most of the document seemed to be complete gibberish. One looked like someone was trying to learn the alphabet. AGCT et cetera. Maybe Lilly was an alien who spoke a strange language. Pausing to laugh at this funny image, James then opened a drawer and found a black notebook. He had heard about Little Black Books and hoped that this had nothing to do with that. It appeared to be a diary. The first entry was at least a few years old. Wow. He really did not know the true Lilly. Among the entries, he noticed the date when he came into Lilly's life. She started out saying what a hunk of a man he was and progressed to the I-wish-he-gave-me-more-action stage. James thought it was Lilly who was constantly looking to go to sleep. He would never understand women. Maybe he should take some estrogen pills for awhile and see if that gave him any insight. Then he remembered Lilly talking about hormone replacement and how women get their features from the hormones they have. Knowing for sure that he didn't want curvy hips and big boobs, James scratched that idea off his mental list. Another recent entry was titled *Lovers Lost in Bliss*. James hadn't realized Lilly wrote short stories and decided to see if it would give him any insight into Lilly's mind.

{Penelope was sitting at her kitchen table munching on a donut and stirring her coffee. She was thinking about her beautiful daughter Calypso. Her bright blue eyes glowed with love for every flower and sprout she came across. Calypso wanted to be the world's most brilliant botanist. Penelope lost the apple of her eye last year in the biggest fire that town had ever seen. The old Munston barn was a hang out for kids. Sometimes they would go there after school to talk and other times it became cancer corner. Most of the time there was a bunch of kids there, but the accident took place when Calypso got there before her friends. Some older kids had just got done having a smoke and decided to go to the ice cream joint. All the kids dropped their cigarettes and jumped on their bikes to get some rocky road. It just so happened that Calypso was up in the loft while a small flame started in the hay. It grew bigger without her notice and eventually engulfed the barn with no means of escape.

Penelope's mind was stuck on that event day after day and her terrible depression kept growing worse. Her boss at work was ready to fire her for her showing up late and poor work ethic. She never wrote the newspaper articles on time and tended to be a glum influence on the others workers. Penelope decided to move somewhere tropical; she was convinced that it was in her best interest to get away from the frigid Canadian life. Her house had just been bought and she had just finished putting most of her useless items on eBay. She had numerous dolls and other such collectibles that had no practical purpose. She had plans to go to Mexico, where a sister had a vacation home. Her kind sister advised her to go to Mexico and get out of the rut she was in. Penelope was excited about the opportunity to leave Canada and spend some time painting. Loving drawing scenic pictures and portraits, Penelope was looking forward to having the inspiration of new landscapes and a new culture of people. She was looking forward to the food...Oh, she could hardly wait to have authentic salsa, and tacos, and other such new finds.

It was a fortnight until most of her stuff had sold and been shipped out. She now had enough money to pick up her life and move. Penelope got a taxi to the airport; she had prearranged her tickets online. Security was a little tight, so they made her take off her high heels and demanded to search through her suitcase. (They even let her pantyhose and underwear fall out on the floor.) She made it through security and had arrived with plenty of time to chill in the waiting area. As she was recovering from the embarrassment of the underwear episode, she took out her book and began where she had left off a month or so ago.

The story was about a couple living in Spain. The wife came down with a rare disease when she had visited Africa. Her husband nursed her back to health with his constant concern, prayers, and loving care. Penelope hoped for a man like that. The last bum she was married to for three years left her when she became pregnant. He was too immature to have kids and went who knows where to party and burn out the rest of his life. Penelope raised Calypso on her own with the help of a single parent support group.

As she was engrossed in her novel, a fine looking young man sat down next to her. He was obviously successful in business; he had a fancy suit and a luxurious watch on. Penelope's heart was imagining a man somewhat like him to sweep her off her feet. She noticed that he did not have a wedding ring on. He caught her interest. She fearlessly leaned over and asked the man if he was seeing someone. Startled, he answered in a suave voice, that "I myself am looking for someone special." Energy rushed through Penelope's body. The two new friends started chatting. He introduced himself as Mr. Seltzer, a stock market man, who had struck it rich by investing in Enron. He said that such close associates could call each other by first names.

He offered that his first name was Alka; Penelope offered her name.

"Alka, what caused you to go into the stock market? It seems like such a risky job."

"Oh, well, I have always been very skilled in mathematics and so I double majored in Statistics and Economics. I knew that I could beat the system with my intuition and talent."

Penelope took all this to mean that he was an intelligent man with a slight case of an inflated ego. She was alright with that. Wanting her man to think well of himself and be self-sufficient, this was a plus. Much better than a man who was too timid to even acknowledge his accomplishments.

"You seem to be a well-off guy."

"I consider myself lucky."

"Where do you happen to be traveling?"

"I am going to Mexico City to meet a man for a stock trade."

All of the sudden, a plane coming in for a landing crashed into the lobby where the two lovers were and burned them up in an explosion.}

James was stunned by the symbolism. He knew that Lilly had some deep emotions, but to see them take shape was another matter. Is our relationship heading for disaster? James also realized that Lilly was also exploring the pain of losing a sibling. Lilly had told him that when she was a kid, her parents gave birth to a still born. Ever since then, Lilly was afraid of the possibility of suffering the same devastation if she had a baby. Thinking professional help was needed, James determined that he would insist on counseling for couples when he found Lilly.

~Hey, James. Look what I found.

It was totally unfair that ranger Rick controlled the show. James decided to pocket the diary and give it a look over when he had some spare time.

~It appears Lilly was writing a letter of resignation. Look at that line right there. "I regret to inform you that I am moving on to start my own lab. I have recently come upon some discoveries that I need to focus full time on. Being in a community of fellow scientists who need my help can become rather distracting. I will be sure to keep in touch. Farewell to my colleagues at The National Center for Biological Studies."

~Lilly never said a word about this decision to me.

5~Thanatos

Back at the funeral home, Zhang was busy filling Lilly in on all the other details. Chi had a tight rein on her and it did not seem that she would be able to escape, even while she was on the outside gathering her materials. Lilly's only hope was to obey Zhang so well that he would begin to trust her. When she had fully gained his trust, and he gave her some freedom, she would flee even if it killed her. Her hatred for Mr. Chi had to be unseen, buried deep until the right moment. If she was lucky, she could leave some type of secret message for James. Her heart was breaking at the thought of what Zhang told her to tell James. The harshness of Chi's message made Lilly's fighting with James seem petty. Just as Mr. Chi was finishing his spiel on obedience, Lilly had the urge to go to the bathroom.

~Mr. Chi, would you excuse me to go to the restroom?

~Yes. Right down that hallway to the left, first door.

Lilly stumbled to the bathroom and the guys wondered if she was sick. Her sickness was of the heart. Knowing that her discovery would go to benefit men just like Zhang was exactly what she most feared. Her plan had been to prepare messages for the world media, go into temporary hiding, and then disseminate her magical pills. The world would go crazy trying to find Lilly, but she would only reveal herself to the pure hearted. She would leave clues and messages that only holy men, women, and children would find. Lilly would totally change her appearance, and would travel throughout the world with her pills, and give them only to the innocent. Children would be her main goal. Her hope was that removal of the death gene would keep the children young and in a state of innocence. Slowly, all evil men and women would die out and Eden would again return to earth. The Thanatos gene would forever be eliminated from the human genome. No one would even know what Thanatos meant.

Lilly knew that her ambitions were magnificent, but with changing her DNA, she would also live forever. Lilly knew that extreme natural disasters like earthquakes could still kill people, but at least they would have time to overcome these forces of nature eventually. Men and women would truly control and have dominion over the earth.

All of this was speculation, but Lilly knew in her heart that this would be possible. The first human test would happen soon enough, and there was no way anything could go wrong. Lilly had checked over her calculations; she knew that biologically the body would completely and naturally accept this alteration.

While in the bathroom daydreaming about the possibilities, Lilly was brought back to the present reality. She decided that she would be the first to take her pill and that there was no time to give it to an elderly patient. Even though reversing death with someone already in old age would prove her success, she did not have time for this. Lilly had no worries that her pill would have any side effects. She gave only the briefest thought to the possibility that it might cause her harm. But she needed to take this pill now. Luckily, Lilly had a few pills made up and stored in an interior coat pocket. While locked in the bathroom, she popped the Pills of Life into her mouth and used the faucet to get some water to wash them down. Truly, springs of living water would flow from her. In only a few hours, death would never have a hold on Lilly. Her grandpa would be so proud.

Zhang Chi began to bang on the bathroom door.

~Lilly. Are you messing around in there?

~I am just washing my hands. I will be out in a second.

~I'm waiting.

Lilly turned on the faucet to convince him of running water. The handle squeaked as she brought the flow to a stop.

She opened the door and saw the dreadful face of her wicked master. He didn't know that she had just set in motion the first miracle of its kind.

~Lilly, you are going to carry out all I told you to do.

Walking obediently back into the garage, she sat in the back seat. Mac and Bob must have cleared out the body of Anna earlier and they were now waiting for her in the front of the car.

~Mac, what are you going to do with Anna's body?

~We put it down in the basement for you to show us what an autopsy looks like. When you get back to your new home, you will provide us with some entertainment. Bob and I have dreamed of being doctors of the living, but all we can manage is to take care of the dead. We want to see how a professional would go about a surgery. This would be a fake surgery, of course. The patient is already dead.

Lilly was instantly sickened at the thought of having to cut open her friend. Worrying that she would vomit, Lilly used all of her might to focus on pleasant imagery. Putting the car in gear, and opening the garage door with the click of a button, Mac pulled out of the garage and on to the road. Lilly didn't feel as comfortable as when James was driving; Mac seemed to be a lazy driver. James had taken an extra class while in school on defensive driving. Mac seemed to disregard all the rules of the road. Plenty of other cars simply got out of the way.

Lilly knew that she had to leave James some type of message, but that she would have to make it short. It would also have to be cryptic in case Bob or Mac came upon it. She knew that James was talented at solving word puzzles, so she tried to come up with a way of giving James the greatest amount of information in as few words as possible. The right words fell into place and she would be ready to write them down.

Lilly was surprised that they did not even have to ask for directions to her house. They truly had been keeping an eye on her already and they would have kidnapped her soon enough. Mac pulled into Lilly's driveway and reminded her of a few key points of the plan. Lilly hoped that James would be home. She pulled the key out of her pocket, unlocked the house, and disarmed the alarm. She pretended to check all the rooms for stray paper work, but was in reality checking for her boyfriend. No luck.

~I just have to go into my office to get a few things.

Lilly found a pile of books that she really didn't need, but could use to give her some time. She would make Bob and Mac carry the books out to the car while she left a Post-it note on her desktop.

~Mac, Bob, could you carry a few books out to the car for me while I gather a few more things?
~Sure, Ma'am.

Bob said this with a politeness that surprised Lilly. Mac followed suit and carried a rather large part of the stack to the car. Lilly would have to write quickly, as they were finishing the job much faster than she had planned. She scribbled down what she had planned beforehand.

–James, bye. Gone to golden sleep. Sleep no more.–

Lilly hoped that James would be able to decode this; Mac had just finished carrying out the last stack and was coming back. Lilly stuck the note to her computer. A split second later and she would have been caught. Mac was at the door frame.
~You remember that we have all your computer files, right?
~Yes, Mac.
~Well, I don't care if you're done here or not. Bob and I are hungry for a burger and we thought it wise to wait until after dark to go to the lab. We don't want anyone to see us carrying out all that junk you need.

The three traveled over to the nearest McDonalds. Mac thought it smart to go through the drive-through, and park and eat. Not caring what type of burger everyone wanted, Mac ordered five Quarter Pounders. Two each for the men and one for the little lady. They parked under a streetlight near a gas station, and Bob went in to get some booze. Figuring that he would become a colleague of Lilly, Mac decided that he should make the best of the situation.
~Zhang's not that bad once you get to know him.
~I think the only reason you think that way is because he provides you with food, shelter, and money. You know that he would be nothing if nobody worked for him. It makes me wonder why a nice guy like you, Mac, would get caught up with Mr. Chi.
~Well, I was homeless and he offered me a job. How could I resist getting off the streets?
~Are you telling me you could find no other job?
~Well. Umm. You see. Mr. Chi was offering a better wage than any other place I found. I could have worked at a fast food restaurant, but Zhang's job opportunity was much sweeter.
~So you never think of leaving Zhang?

~No, not really. But I'm sure you're trying to figure out a way to escape. That is why Zhang has us keep such a tight hold on you. I have never seen him want what someone has so bad. I have to admit, I would like to take some of your pills. But you make it sound like more testing has to be done first. I guess that is why Zhang wants to keep you. If he could manufacture the pills on his own, he would dispose of you faster than a Venus Flytrap bites its prey.

~That is a lovely thought.

~I thought you would enjoy the imagery.

Returning from the gas station with a six pack, Bob passed a beer to Mac and told Lilly that she did not need any alcohol. Lilly felt that some alcohol might help calm her nerves, but she did not want to argue. The three finished their burgers and waited a while longer for dark.

6~Creativity

James and Rick finished up in Lilly's office and they still hadn't figured out where she was. James feared the worst, but Rick remained hopeful.

~Come on, James. Maybe she went to a meeting in another city and was not able to make it back.

~Rick, she would have called.

~Do you have an answering machine?

~Yes. How 'bout we go home and check that out.

The two made their way from the third floor to the ground floor and out on to the street. James had always dreamed of driving a cop car and thought that maybe Rick would give him the chance to fulfill that wish.

~Hey. Rick. Do you think I could drive?

~That's not protocol, but I guess you could just this once.

~Thanks, man!

James was ecstatic and hopped right over to the driver's seat. Rick handed him the keys and made a silent petition to God that He keep them both alive. Their journey back to James house was successful.

~James, I have to get back to the station. I'll try to keep working on finding Lilly. You do the same.

~Thanks for your company today.

~Sure, no problem.

Home was quiet and dark. Going over to the couch, James remembered the diary in his pocket. Curiosity again took hold of him. Turning to a random page, James saw a poem entitled Fire.

Fire
Hot
burning
light
heat
keep the enemy away
camping with you my friend
hearts aglow
candles lit
yellow orange and purple
white and red fireworks
hot dogs in a pan
boiling water overflowing
the sun millions of miles away
moon reflecting the electromagnetism of the sun
other stars are showing that they are just as bright
alpha centauri what a sight
pollution clouding the sight of the fire
the fire in the sky
the dome of God
sitting upon the mountain of fire
poor little children cold and tired
fire we need you to work hard for us
powering people
calorie counting
little units of heat
refine this metal
make it pure
weld a wire
fire fighters try to bite it
lapping flames upon the hearth
houses burned up or down
never sideways
other planets need their own warmth

the rich coal will expire
bombs and blasts and burning masts
love and hate in a fire of rage
wild forests burnt to the ground
river of life dried
ring of fire taking me down
satan and his angels bound
in the eternal flame will burn
down down down
never to return
lift your head up
you do not have to go there
choose life love and happiness
from Jesus our Savior
river of life wash the pain away
heal my wounds and make me okay
walking side by side the Light
no need for sun or moon or stars
for the Lamb is bright
God in His glory
completely divine
ages past and ages future
we will spend in love together
friendship never to be severed
Fire of Life
You are the Light of the World
Holy Spirit on Pentecost ablaze
come and rest your fire on us
light our hearts with love for all
bring us to be great and tall
but only grand in the way of peace
show us anew how you created
all there is with none defeated
renew all things and show your glory
turn us to your perfect ways
light our path throughout our days
thank you for your perfect life
you shed your blood for our forgiveness
what can we do but sing your praises

forever ringing true
Light of the world
you shine before us
The Everlasting FIRE

Not too shabby for a scientist. Wondering how well James could compare in a poetic endeavor, he grabbed a pen and let his creative juices flow.

alone in a dark wood
breathing heavy
perspiring
beads of sweat roll down my brow
eyes of red give me a scowl
my heart beats louder
my ears scream
my nose runs
my eyes refuse to turn away
my hands freeze over with fear
the wolf is coming to eat me
he wants me in his stomach
I do not want to go there

In his self critique, James thought his ending rather lame. He crumpled up the poem and tossed it in the garbage. One more try and then he would call it quits.

Money
the lord of men
ever controlling
never fulfilling
happiness promising
always losing
store up your gain
only to lose it tomorrow
used to buy things
get it when you sell things
only a piece of worthless paper
Okay, Lilly. You win. I suck at poetry. James got up to go to the

fridge, but felt drawn in a different direction. Making his way to Lilly's home office, James saw the note stuck to the top of the computer screen. His mind was boggled over how that got there, because he was sure it was not there before. Taking a closer look, James realized it was from Lilly.

–James, bye. Gone to golden sleep. Sleep no more.–

James was unsure why it was unclear. His only conclusion was that it must have be written cryptically for some reason. James sat down in the office chair and pondered. How did this get here during the day? Lilly had been gone since early morning. Hmm. Reading the note aloud to himself, James realized some interesting connections between the sounds. Sleep no more sounded like S'more. Hmm. And the gold reminded him of what was stuffed down Joey's throat. James remembered how when a character died in the Bible, it was said that they went to sleep. Or when someone slept with someone else, that meant they had sex. James thought that the death definition was a more probable connection as it tied with the gold. Taking away the S from sleep left a seeming connection to leap. Did that mean he was supposed to go where there was S' mores. Hmm. And then the "gone to golden sleep." Did that mean go to a graveyard? Lilly's hand writing looked sloppy and that only happened when she was in a hurry. Otherwise, she wrote with the best trained penmanship that James had ever seen.

By the time James had finished trying to figure out the note, it was late at night. He was terribly concerned about Lilly, but he knew that if he did not get a restful night of sleep, he would be fatigued in the morning. His hope was that he would wake up and Lilly would be back home cooking breakfast. If this wish didn't come true, he would dedicate his whole day to finding Lilly. He had some hunches as to what the note meant. Tomorrow he would find out if they were right.

7~Pills

The cover of darkness had fallen.

~Lilly, I hope you have been thinking through the list of items that you are going to need from the lab.

Mac spouted out with an air of condescension.

Lilly was lucky that she always carried an extra electronic entry card to the lab in a zippered pocket in the inside of her coat. She was afraid that if she did not have that, Mac and Bob would find a way to break into the lab. She did not want any damage to the lab. If Mac broke in, the alarm would go off, they would flee, and Lilly would not get any of her equipment. She was sure that Mr. Chi would be extremely agitated if they did not accomplish their mission. Zhang seemed to be a man with a short fuse and even less patience.

The van screeched to a halt in front of the lab. Maybe someone nearby would realize that Lilly was being held hostage, but it seemed unlikely at this hour of the night. Everyone would be in their secure home watching American Idol. Lilly wondered how a supposedly Christian country could become so obsessed over this blatant idolatry. The exaltation of man for his singing ability with no thanks to God was a terrible sin. The proper object of admiration and worship is God. The book of Revelation tells how all of the universe worships God in song. Angels continually surround Him declaring His power, wisdom, beauty, and goodness.

Mac put the car in park, turned it off, opened the rusty door, and jumped out.

~Bob, Lilly. Hurry up! We don't have all night. Mr. Chi wants us back before midnight.

Bob had some reservations.

~Ok, Mac. I'm still trying to settle the beer and burgers in my stomach from the roller coaster ride that you just put us through.

~Bob, you really need to control your eating habits.

~What do you mean, Mac? You ate the same food I did.

~Yeah, well, you see, I took at least twice as long to eat it. That gives your body more time to adjust to the increase of material. You eat like it's going out of style. We should call you the vacuum cleaner.

~That's hilarious, Mac. Haha.

~Boys! Can we just get my stuff?

~Sure.

Lilly was not sure why she had this sudden urge to get her equipment. Being tired of male jokes might have something to do with it. The company of three made their way up to the door and Lilly swiped her entry card. The sound of the locking mechanism disengaging could be heard. The door popped open and Lilly led the way inside. She considered trying to lock them in a lab room, for the doors only opened by card on both sides. Lilly thought that might be too risky at this point in the game. She remembered that she was going to try to gain Zhang's trust first. The elevator ride up to the third floor was punctuated with an inside joke between Mac and Bob. Lilly almost wished that one of them was a woman; this would keep the crude jokes to a minimum. But, Lilly knew some pretty crass females.

Lilly led the way to her office and the lab that was adjacent to it. She figured that she would need some beakers, Erlenmeyer flasks, petri dishes, pipettes, and other common paraphernalia.

~Mac, Bob. You were so great at gathering the books at my house that I thought you could help with the lab equipment. Just go into the room right here and grab two of each type of dishware.

Mac responded with one hesitation.

~Ma'am. We can handle it, but this time one of us is going to stay with you. We want to make sure you don't try to leave some type of note. Mr. Chi warned me how women can be cunning and deceitful. We let this precaution slip while we were at your house. Don't think we didn't realize that. But we figured that you didn't have anytime between our trips to the car to leave a note, right?

Mac questioned with suspicion.

~Of course I didn't leave a note.

Lilly responded with false sincerity.

~Good.

Somewhat reassured, Mac went to the lab first, found an empty box in the corner, and started filling it with glassware. Bob hung around Lilly's office, while Lilly looked for her journal. Missing. Odd. Nobody should have access to my office. Lilly sorted through her stack of articles, data sheets, and personal notes, and found the specific papers she was looking for. Mac had already made a trip down to the van and back and was telling Bob what type of items to take.

Lilly had a quick moment to herself while the two of them were in the lab. She reached into a bottom drawer, found the bottle of pills she was looking for, and stuck the container into her coat pocket. These were not Pills of Life. Malevolent thoughts raced through Lilly's mind. If only she could get these men to ingest these pills. A brilliant idea arose in her mind. She would tell them they were The Pills of Life, when in reality, they caused death in a little over seven minutes. She kept these pills in case any of the animals she was working on needed to be exterminated. Mac slyly crept into the back of Lilly's office and surprised Lilly with a tap on the shoulder. Lilly let out a scream that was heard, but not heeded.

~Quiet, Lilly! I was just playing a joke.

~Mac! I swear if you ever do that again... I'll....

~What will you do? Huh? I didn't think so. Bob and I run the show. Got it?

~Yes, Mac. Just don't give me a heart attack.

~You're young and healthy. Why would you be worried about a heart attack?

~Mac, a heart attack can happen to anybody.

~Really? You don't say. I'm going to go sneak up on Bob next. Maybe then it will just be the two of us, sugar pie.

Disgusting. Lilly was completely repulsed. She was definitely not his sugar anything. An image of James grilling steak and potatoes for a romantic dinner flashed into Lilly's mind. She would give anything to be back in James' arms.

Finally, all the supplies and paperwork were packed into the van. Lilly said a silent goodbye to the lab. She hoped that she would soon be back as a free woman. Everybody climbed into the van. They were headed to the place of the dead.

8~Dreams

Cheerful birds were singing as James awoke from a fitful nights sleep. Horrific dreams of 20/20 shows that he had seen flashed before his mind all night long. One particularly vivid and distressing scene was that of a pregnant 24 year-old being abducted while she was taking a walk in her neighborhood. The pervert that captured her was later found out by following a trail of drug transactions.

James longed with all his heart for Lilly to be in the kitchen making a pot of coffee. Slipping on slippers, gingerly walking over to the bathroom to take care of some personal relief, and then shuffling down the hall, James found an empty house. There was no trace of any recent human activity. The somber reality of only having a note to figure out where Lilly was sank into his heart. James let out a gasp and plea to God to help him find his girl before the ultimate danger of death found her. James was not used to praying and was not even sure who he was praying to at the moment. He had just seen a poll in the newspaper that said that even atheists utter prayers in times of desperation. This was one of those times.

~Help me to find Lilly and let no torture of any kind be afflicted upon her, Lord.

James strode over to Lilly's office to recover the note.

–James, bye. Gone to golden sleep. Sleep no more.–

The only way he found to logically connect all the sounds of the note led him to a spot in town where he and Lilly always went to get s'more flavored ice-cream. This particular ice-cream parlor was located adjacent to a funeral home, fulfilling the "sleep no more" line. Unsure of whether or not to call Rick, James decided that he wanted to be the one who recovered Lilly and he would seem a fool if Lilly was not there.

Realizing that he should at least look decent, James went to take a quick shower. While in the shower singing an off key version of "My Humps," James thought about the intimate times he and Lilly spent together in the hot steam. One event in particular filled all his senses. He experienced it again as if it were happening.

{He stared with longing into the seductive eyes of Lilly. She wanted him real bad. She stuck her tongue in his mouth like a bear licking honey. Their lips squished. Waves of lust and desire swept through them and permeated their beings.}

Before he knew it, ice cold water started falling on him. He had been in the shower so long that all the hot water in their tank had been used up. He reached out to the faucet and turned it off before he became totally frozen. What a harsh dose of reality. Getting out and toweling off, James wished his fantasy was real again. In order to be comfortable, James pulled on his loose, tattered jeans and his Joey Mullen's jersey.

All set for the day, James headed out to the car and was surprised by an abrupt dog bark. James scanned the area. No dog in sight.

9~Eden

Lilly awoke in a foreign place. She didn't remember falling asleep there. Clearing her eyes, she turned around and saw Zhang poised in a chair staring into her soul. Shivers ran down her back like lightning.

~Good morning, Ms. Summer. Would you like a cup of coffee?

~Please.

~Sugar or milk?

~Black is fine.

~Scientists like it strong, don't they? Staying up late at night doing experiments overexerts the hypothalamus. I knew of a lady who drank five pots of coffee a day. She ended up here at the age of 43. The body is just not meant to be subjected to so much caffeine. In her case, caffeine wasn't the only killer, but we don't have to go into that now.

Feeling queasy from this threatening tale, Lilly was rethinking the coffee, but decided that she was too thirsty to refuse any liquids.

~Here you go.

~Thank you for the java, Zhang.

~I have been thinking about your Project Thanatos.

~What about it?

~Silence! Let me finish. I have determined that I am going to give you a half hour to finish any last minute testing and then you are going to give me a Pill of Life.

~It seems that I have no choice in the matter.

~That is correct, Ms. Summer. All your equipment has been placed in the room to your left. All your files are contained on the PC in the corner. I will be back in thirty minutes to take my elixir.

Lilly scrambled to find her coat. She needed to get the Pills of Death. Luckily, her coat was draped over the side of the couch and both types of pills were contained therein. She decided that the situation was as easy as getting everyone to take the Pills of Death. She was glad that the pills were not instantaneous in their killing, because Zhang might make Bob or Mac take them first to see if there were any immediate side effects. Lilly kept it simple by having one container in each of her front pockets. She decided that she should look like she was running final tests, so she booted up the computer and ran a diagnostic program. Bob wandered into the room.

~Hey, Lilly. Mr. Chi is ecstatic about taking your pill.

~That's encouraging to hear.

~Well, I was just looking for Mac. Zhang wants to thank us for all our hard work for him by letting us take the pills first. You haven't seen him, have you?

~No.

~Maybe he went next door to have some ice cream. I'm going to go check and then be right back.

~Ok, Bob. See you in a bit. And by the way, all the final tests are running perfect.

Staring off into space waiting for the half hour to pass by, Lilly started thinking about her Utopia. The name of her project came from the Greek word for death, Thanatos. She thought it proper that Thanatos would be forever eliminated.

She wondered what God thought about her plans. Was it the job of humanity or God to bring back Eden? Lilly had wondered about this off and on most of her life. A garden seemed a perfect merger between the science of biology and the spirit of God. God's first job for man was to be a gardener. Lilly knew in her heart that she was still serving God by caring for His garden of humans. Perfect harmony seemed possible. Lilly envisioned the last few verses of The Book of Revelation.

"And he shewed me a pure river of water of life, clear as crystal, proceeding out of the throne of God and of the Lamb. In the midst of the street of it, and on either side of the river, was there the tree

of life, which bare twelve manner of fruits, and yielded her fruit every month: and the leaves of the tree were for the healing of the nations."

Lilly dreamed that her Pills of Life were like the Tree of Life. Mankind missed their opportunity the first time, but Lilly was going to make sure they accepted it today.

While in her fantasy, the door to the room opened.

10~Life & Death

Bob and Zhang entered the room with a look of greed in their eyes. Zhang deceptively told Bob to accept the first Pill of Life. Lilly reached slowly into the pocket that had the Pills of Death, heart-broken at what she was about to do. She wondered if Mac would come in. She hoped he would not mess up the plan. Bob put his hand forward and accepted the pill from Lilly. Lilly gave a weak smile and Bob's eyes twinkled with evil intentions. He popped the pill. There was no turning back now. She wondered what Bob would have done if he had lived forever. Bob began to look enlightened. He shared his thoughts with Chi.

~Zhang, I feel fine. I actually feel better than fine. I feel like rivers of life are coursing through my veins.

Zhang could stand it no longer.

~Lilly, I'll take my pill now.

She was glad that Zhang was taking it before Bob started to die. Both men took deep breaths of air like they were new born infants. Lilly was preparing herself for what would happen in a few minutes.

Suddenly, Bob started gasping and Zhang started coughing. Lilly reassured them that it was their body expelling germs. Bob started to turn blue. Zhang vomited. Bob lost control of his bladder and peed himself. Without warning, both men fell to the floor like bricks. Their lives were now over.

Lilly felt waves of guilt. The act was in self defense, but it still made her a killer. While in a cloud of confusion, Lilly was startled when Mac opened the door. He stepped into the room and instantly realized all was not right.

~What have you done, Lilly?

~I don't know. They just fell over.

~Did you give them any of your pills?

~No. They wanted to wait until you arrived to take the pills. Maybe they are having a severe reaction to the homemade clam chowder they both just ate.

~Whatever happened, I really don't care. But I do want to take one of your Pills of Life.

~Okay. Here's the bottle. Lilly handed him the full bottle of the Pills of Death.

~Lilly, dear. I want to see you try them first.

Mac offered her back one of the killer pills. Lilly feared for her life, but realized she had taken a Pill of Life just a day ago. This was the ultimate test.

~Sure, Mac. I would be glad to have the pleasure.

Lilly popped the pill and waited to feel any different. Five minutes passed and there were still no changes. Another five minutes and Mac was satisfied that the pill did not kill. Lilly's spirit uttered a fervent prayer in thanks to God. She was still alive.

~Here goes nothing, doll.

Mac gulped down the pill and went over to the fridge to get a beer to wash it down.

~Lilly, I am impressed. I feel blood running through my body like it never has before. You're a genius.

~Thank you, Mac.

Mac was laughing in ecstasy; someone stepped through the door into the basement. It was James. Giving a brief look at Lilly, James turned to Mac. Startled, Mac pulled out a gun and was ready to fire, but James beat him to it with a gun of his own. A loud blast was heard and blood started leaking out of Mac onto the floor. James motioned to Lilly to get out of the basement, and they both escaped into the fresh air.

Lilly's mind gushed with thoughts.

~James. I was so worried that I would never see you again. I was so scared. James. I love you. Never leave me.

~Lilly, calm down. Everything is alright. You're safe now. Nobody's going to harm you.

The two lovers gave each other a passionate kiss of reunion.

~James, I am so glad you brought a gun. I was afraid Mac was going to shoot you. I never thought my Project Thanatos would cause so much trouble.

~What are you talking about, Lilly?

~I'll tell you more about it when we get home.

~Promise?

~Yes. But, James, what should we do about the dead guys down there?

~I've gotten to be pretty good friends with Rick and I think that he will be able to take care of this. That is if you are able to explain to him why the three guys are dead.

~I think that will take quite a bit of explaining.

~How much?

~Well, James, let's just say I could write a book.

11~A New Life

The rain was unexpected but no matter, Lilly was twirling in happiness. Her long time boyfriend had proposed to her and promised his faithfulness forever. How could Lilly resist? Today had been their wedding and the storm overhead was merely a distraction. Her life would become more solid and stable now that she had a man whom she could always depend on. Just recently, with her discovery, her husband became even more protective of her. She was glad. The last mess she was in might have been her end if it were not for James. He rescued her like a knight from a fable. No one else but James knew about Lilly's secret project.

Before God Almighty she had promised herself to James and he to her. The church building had been full of friends. James had his rich parents sitting up in the first row and Lilly had her aged Mother and atheist brother, Tim. Mary Summer could not be more proud of her daughter. She sat there gleaming with joy and pride.

Throughout Mary's life there had been many troubles. As an adolescent, Lilly could be quite a trouble maker. Lilly was not content with being a nurse, but wanted to be a top notch biologist. Mary demanded that she either be a nurse or a teacher and Lilly firmly denied either choice. Constantly experimenting with her lab set, peering into a microscope, and dissecting frogs turned off Lilly's mother. Mary wanted Lilly to babysit younger children or read books about an adventuresome nurse. Leaving all these wishes in the past, Mary was overwhelmed with Lilly's accomplishments.

Ken and Cara Clark were glad that the longtime couple finally tied the knot. Ken had been starting to worry that James would not step up and be a man.

The whole church arose while Lilly and James strode out of the chapel into their car with cans tied on the back bumper. Lilly requested that they be beer cans in remembrance of two people who she did not want to forget, but that she was silently glad were dead.

Lilly's mind flashed back to the day when James found her in a funeral home with two dead bodies and a vicious man ready to shoot him. With his quick instincts, James brought along a gun and made the call to shoot the man before the man shot him. Lilly was grateful to James for her life. He told her that they were going to have to tell the police about these murders right away. James gave Lilly the phone to call Rick Pritchard and fill him in on the incident. She managed to keep out what exactly her discovery was and yet explain that these men kidnapped her in order to have her knowledge.

Amazingly, Rick respected that she did not want to tell the exact nature of her research. Rick said he had enough sway at the police department that he would be able to explain this to his boss as a kidnapping. No more details would be needed. Rick arrived at the scene and saw the bodies lying on the floor. With one quizzical look at Lilly, Rick called in to his boss and reported the self-defense case of Lilly Summer and James Clark. Rick's boss immediately came down to the scene also and had some penetrating questions. James was able to convince the Chief that Lilly was extremely exhausted and needed time to recover. James left Rick and the Chief to take care of the details.

Getting Lilly into the car, James drove her home, and sat her down on the couch and asked if she was able to explain thoroughly what just happened. Lilly spilled her whole tale to James and he sat their with a piercing stare of disbelief. When Lilly got to the part in the story where she took the toxin, James fully believed Lilly. How else could she survive unless her discovery was real? James took Lilly in his arms and gave her an embrace like no other. Lilly truly felt the depth of James' love. Right there in their living room, James knelt down and proposed to Lilly without a ring in hand. Lilly knew this was her man. Yes. Yes. Again and again she would tell him that they were meant for each other.

Lilly knew the character of James' heart in that he did not ask for a Pill of Life for himself, but only questioned what type of biological change went on in Lilly's body. Lilly knew that she could safely offer James a Pill of Life and James paused and asked God to bless their coming union and long life. Staring at the pill, James considered well what he was doing with his body, and his complete trust of Lilly reassured him that this was the plan.

Filling James in on the next phase of her mission was even more exhilarating. He was all for traveling the world with her magic potion. Now that they were married, they would sell all they have, and journey to Northern Wisconsin. James parents had a cabin up there that he knew they never used anymore. The issue of not explaining to his parents where he was did not bother James. Lilly reassured James that there was always the possibility of visiting them unannounced and that they could set up P.O. boxes around the country.

The two love birds were ready for a new life together.

12~Guns

One week after the wedding, James and Lilly had an auction for their house and belongings arranged. In the week between the end of their wedding and the auction day, they made plenty of plans for their trip.

Lilly issued her letter of resignation to her lab partners and James told his parents that he was going on a long trip and might not see them for a while. The new Clark family promoted their house and belongings for sale so that there would be a large group of people to bid and win their stuff. The auctioneer rattled off nonsense like no other person James had ever heard.

~50 dolla 50. 50 dolla. 75 dolla. Yes, Ma'am. Number 23 wins. Now onto the couch and cushions.

~Lilly, I sure hope we make enough money to travel.

James said this with sincerity. Lilly responded with exuberant confidence.

~James. Calm down. We only need enough money to get started and then people will be more than willing to donate to our cause.

~You're right, Lilly, I'm being a wart.

~Honey, I can take care of that wart for you. I have the perfect cream.

James looked at Lilly with an unsure glance. Lilly chuckled and picked up a box of paintings that they were selling and set it up on a table so that people could see more closely the caliber of the artist. All their stuff was numbered and James was sad to see his hockey paraphernalia disappear.

Lilly was frenzied and exhausted and James was the same by the end of the day. Lilly had specified for the auction that it all be carried out with cash so that the couple would be able to leave right away with money in hand. James had arranged for a vault to be secured to their car and they stashed all their earnings into its secure container. James had just checked their car for any possible problems, changed the oil, and filled up the tank with premium gas.

By 7PM that same night, James and Lilly were on the road for Northern Wisconsin. James drove since he knew the way and had been up to the cabin a few times as a kid. James leaned over to whisper in Lilly's ear.

~Sugar pie, I love you.

~Oh, James. You're a hopeless romantic. And I cannot resist, but we will have to wait for the comfy north woods bed.

James left eyebrow rose with anticipation. Lilly had been drinking too much coffee and asked James to pull over at a gas station. Scurrying in, Lilly went to the womens' room but found it occupied, shyly she went to the mens' door and knocked. No reply. The door was not locked. She hurried in to find a man at the urinal. Lilly was not sure if she should leave or go to the toilet pretending she was a man. Her bladder made the decision. As Lilly was closing the door to the toilet the man turned and looked her in the eye. The man's jaw dropped.

~What the hell are you doing in here?

~Sorry, sir, but I need a toilet.

Closing the door and sitting down, Lilly hoped no more questions would be asked, but the man had other plans. He stood next to the partition and carried on the conversation.

~So, little lady, what brings you to this gas station?

~Umm. Sir, can I finish first?

~No. I want to know. Other wise I will look under the door.

~Freak! Don't you dare! I will scream.

~That will make a good story. Woman screaming in the mens' room.

~Ok. I'll tell you why I'm here.

The only reason Lilly could think of was the obvious. Vacation.

~Sir, my husband and I are going up to our cabin.

~And where is your cabin?

~That is none of your business.

~Ma'am. I will peek.

Lilly had no idea how to deal with such an insane guy. What a pervert. Why can't he just leave me alone?

~It's in Phillips, Wisconsin. You happy now?

~Yes.

Hearing that the man went to wash his hands, dry his hands, and use his hands to open the creaky door, Lilly felt that she was safe to leave. She carefully unlocked the door, having the thought that bathroom doors need better latches. She carried out her hygienic needs and left for the safety of James. Her husband was finishing filling the car up with gas and Lilly smiled and jumped into the passenger side.

Putting the nozzle back, James fired up the engine and drove off. Lilly explained to James her freaky encounter.

~James, why are some men such animals?

~Ummm. Lilly. If I told you that, you would run away and become a nun.

~I think I can handle the truth of manhood.

~Okay, Lilly. Here it is. Men are either hungry or horny.

~You've only confirmed what I've already suspected.

Driving along on dark country roads, the couple expected to see few cars, but ever since they had left the gas station a white Ford F350 Crew Cab truck was following them. James was curious, and Lilly was suspicious that it was the same freak from the gas station. Deciding to see if the Ford was following them, James turned off on to the next side road he saw and sure enough the Ford was tailing behind.

Speeding up, James looked for a house that was occupied, but all he found in his quick search was a short driveway with no house. James turned into the driveway, backed out, and backtracked down the road they had just turned on. The Ford slowed down as the Clarks passed, and then eerily u-turned and began following them again. James floored their Toyota Highlander Hybrid, reached the main country road, and sped further along looking for any sign of human life. He hoped to pull up in a person's driveway and knock on the door and explain the situation. If the creeps pursued them at the house, James would be ready to take out his pistol. Luckily, Lilly spotted some lights ahead that turned out to be porch lights. James had been looking in the rear view mirror to keep an eye on how close the maggots were following them. The house was well lit and looked like a safe option for the travelers.

~Lilly, I'm sorry this is happening, but we have to keep our heads on straight. I'm going to pull into the driveway and we are going to get out, and calmly, but quickly, walk up to the door.

~What if the creep follows us?

~Well, I am hoping that the people in the house will take us in, but if not, I have my pistol.

~James! I'm sick and tired of anything having to do with violence and death. You can't seriously be thinking of using a weapon?

~Sweetie. This guy must be after us for some reason, however deluded it might be. What if he is out to harm us? It might come down to either us or him.

The Highlander cruised into the driveway and James and Lilly leapt from the car and scurried up to the porch. After knocking quickly, loudly, and with gusto, the door opened and a fifty year old man appeared and asked who they were and what they wanted.

~Sir. We are being followed by someone who is perhaps dangerous and we are looking for some safety. Could you help us?

~Wow. I've heard lots of crazy stuff, but this has to be at the top of the list. Hurry. Get inside.

Lilly turned around to look out the door as the man was closing it and saw the freak park his car on the side of the road and sit there with his lights on. Spine tingling fear ran through Lilly's body and caused her to let out a shriek mixed with a moan. The home owner reassured Lilly that he was well armed; he was a champion deer hunter.

~Calm down, lady. I have five rifles in the cabinet right there. You can hold one if you like.

Lilly declined, but asked a question.

~Sir, what exactly are we going to do if the man out there tries to get in here?

~I'll pretend that he has wasting disease and blow his head off.

Lilly asked if she could sit down and the gentlemen hospitably affirmed such an action.

~James, dear, could you keep on eye on the street and the gentlemen and I...

~The name is Mike, by the way. Mike O' Donald.

~Lilly. And my husband, James.

~Do you have a last name?

~Summer, errr. Clark. We just got married.

~What a honey moon adventure you're having tonight.

Mike's wife came up from the basement with a scarf she had

been knitting and asked what all the racket was about. Surprised to see two strangers, Mike's wife asked for a detailed explanation.

~Jill, these are our two sudden guests, Lilly and James.

~Pleased to make your acquaintance.

~Same here, Ma'am.

      James replied.

~I'm fine with you calling me Jill.

      She responded with firm kindness.

      James was still peering intently out the window. Unexpectedly, the man in the truck jumped out and started creeping up the driveway.

~MIKE!

      James exclaimed.

~Oh, Lord help us.

      Jill prayed out loud.

      Mike grabbed his rifle.

~Everybody, I'm not going to kill him, I'm just gonna shoot him in the thigh. If he bleeds to death, that is his own fault. A big boy like that should know how to stop his own bleeding.

      BANG!

      Mike blew out the glass from his front door window pane and the creep fell over and screamed like a shemale. Lilly let out a scream of her own.

~Mike. How could you?

      Lilly asked, exasperated at what was happening.

      The man outside cursed at them and slowly crawled back to his truck. He managed to get into his seat. He then honked the horn in anger and frustration. The engine started up and the freak drove away.

~Lilly, I don't think that man will bother you again! That's what he gets for wanting to look up a married woman's dress.

      James said this with a twisted grin.

      Mike slouched back into his favorite chair and started chatting.

~I really hope that man didn't leave a big mess in my yard. If he was familiar with the area, he would just go into Shaana and find the community doctor. And I hope even more that he doesn't convince the cops that we are the criminals for shooting him. Maybe, I was just a little bit rash.

      Jill rolled her eyes and responded.

~Mike, you could say that again. You old coot, but I love you even more for protecting a young couple.

Her motherly instincts kicking in, Jill persuaded everyone to go to bed.

~You two are lucky we have a guest room. Right over there. We can talk more in the morning.

13~Africa

Sirens alarmed the O' Donalds and Clarks at around 7 AM that morning. Mike arose with a start and shot off some profanities, while Jill tried to calm her husband. At the other end of the house Lilly and James whispered to each other. They were unsure over whether they should sneak out or not. They did not want to become entangled with the police. After all, they didn't shoot the man.

~James, we just can't leave them when they saved us.

~Lilly, what happens if the cops blame us or Mike and Jill turn on us?

~You're being too pessimistic. The O' Donalds seem like fine people. You and Mike should go and explain to the cops what happened.

Two police officers knocked on the door. Mike had on checkered pajamas as he opened the door to two men. Jill was in her room getting made up, as was Lilly in her room. James thought he should give Mike some back up. He was surprised to see that one of the cops was Rick. Last James heard, Rick had been promoted to a state cop.

~James, funny that I run into you here. You can't seem to stay away from trouble. I had a hard time explaining away our old mess. Now you get me in a new mess. Please tell me you didn't shoot this guy or I am going to take away your gun or put you in jail. Now, what happened here?

~Rick. Let Mike explain the whole situation.

Unsure of the whole story, Mike asked James a favor.

~James. You explain the background story and I'll explain why I shot the guy.

Rick was taking notes and asked for clarification.

~So it was the homeowner who shot the guy? The police file says this is the home of the O'Donalds. Is that correct?

~Yes, Sir, Rick.

~And that makes you Mike.

~Guilty. I mean innocent. You know what I mean.

~James, buddy, give me the background.

Mr. Clark ran through the whole story and got to the point where he and Lilly arrived at the O'Donalds house. Mike took the story from there. Rick was satisfied with their tale and offered them further details about the situation.

~The man you are referring to is Java Pelushi. He is a diplomat from Africa and wanted to talk to Lilly Summer.

James went to find Lilly finishing primping her hair.

~Honey, you will not believe this. Rick is at the door.

~Are you serious?

~Look for yourself. And he says that the man that Mike shot was Java Pelushi.

~O' Lord, no. Tell me we didn't shoot Java. He's a contact I made from Southern Africa. He read one of my articles on genetics and called me to ask some questions. This was before the episode with Chi. Java and I had been talking for a few weeks already and I told him that I was going up North if he needed to contact me. I really wonder why he would come up here! And then we shot him!

Lilly rushed out of the guest room to talk with Rick. She offered her apologies and asked Rick a question.

~Where is Mr. Pelushi right now?

Rick offered an answer.

~He managed to get to the Shaana hospital. God knows how. He is demanding immediate contact from you for an explanation.

~Rick. James and I will drive over to Shaana as soon as we can.

~Well, Lilly, if you can keep him from pressing charges, this matter could be smoothed out a lot easier. I have been talking to Mike and it looks like he has a few unregistered guns. That also has to be settled. James and Lilly, you are free to go right now, but I will need you to call as soon as you finish with Mr. Pelushi.

The Clark's gave their best wishes and thanks to the O' Donalds and said that they hoped they could meet again in better circumstances. The O' Donald's responded likewise.

Lilly went to the guest room to pack up their belongings, and James stayed out in the living room to catch up with Rick. Calling James into the bedroom, Lilly offered him the suitcases. She would open the doors for him.

~Lilly, you enjoy having me do the heavy lifting, don't you?

~Of course, darling. After all, I'm just a little lady.

The two walked out to their Highlander and James heaved the luggage into the trunk. James climbed into the drivers seat and Lilly lugged herself into shotgun and pulled out a map of Wisconsin in order to find Shaana. The couple had plenty of talking to do. Lilly had to explain tons of details to James in order to get him up to date. Every aspect of their two lives was flying by at an unparalleled pace.

~James, you see how I needed to let a few key people know about Project Thanatos!

~Yes! But you could have told me that you had done so.

~Well, I know I should have. Present circumstances have given us a wonderful opportunity to offer my pill to a patient that has a wound so we can see if the would heals faster than normal. I was going to give the pill to him anyway, once we got to Africa.

Lilly and James arrived in Shaana and found the miniature hospital. They stepped out of their car and entered the infirmary. The receptionist responded that Mr. Pelushi was no longer there and that he did not leave a means of contact. Lilly's gut told her that danger was still in the air. Lilly took out her cell phone and dialed for the African diplomat.

~Java Pelushi speaking.

~O, Lord.

~Who is this?

~This is Lilly. Where are you right now?

~I am in Belowa.

~Java, extremely freaky incidents are happening.

~Please explain.

After at least ten minutes, the real Java was up to date.

~Lilly, I just discovered that some of my shady political opponents have been wire tapping my phone. I highly suspect that one of them is the stalker.

~Java, what are we supposed to do?

~My advice would be to change your travel plans without telling anybody.

~That sounds wise to me. Thank you, Java. Bye.

Lilly's mind churned out a brilliant idea.

~James, let's get in the car.

Once in the Highlander, Lilly rattled off a wild plan.

~We are going to head to the nearest airport and get a plane to Africa. Java has already told me that once we are in his company, he can supply us with guards and monetary support. Java really wants to help the children of Africa.

~Ok, Lilly, let's go ahead.

After consulting the map, driving for forty minutes, registering a flight, waiting in line, and finally boarding the plane, Lilly and James were exhausted. James fell asleep, but Lilly's thoughts kept her from dozing off. She knew that perpetual physical health was now possible, but she could not understand how to change the spirit of man?

The answer to Lilly's question is contained in the life of two men. The first man sinned and every man after him has continued in evil ways. All humans fall short of the glory of God. People lie, steal, cheat and blaspheme God's name; the penalty for sin is death. But one man lived a perfect life. His name is Jesus Christ, and He is both God and man. By living a perfect life, He could take the penalty for our sin. As the perfect Lamb of God, He offered himself up to take the death penalty for us. He paid our fine and by faith in His sacrifice, we can be set free. He showed He conquered death by rising from the dead. If we believe in His death and resurrection, we can inherit eternal life.

82

Believe.

Choose the Pill of Life.

Conquer Thanatos.

The Void

The Full Gospel of John KJV
Interspersed with Assorted Quotes
of Classic Literature and Religious
Texts

Table of Contents

Reflection Questions & Pictures Throughout

All Scripture quotations are taken from the King James Version of the Bible.

SongsofJesus.com sells awesome Christian music and provided the KJV text for The Void.

Visit NewLifeFromHeaven.com to learn more about God.

To explore the full text of the quotes used throughout, view Sacred-Texts.com.

Pictures in The Void can be found at FromOldBooks.org.

How to Go to Heaven
According to the Word of God

It is very simple to be saved and takes only a minute to explain. Please let me show you how to go to Heaven from the Bible, God's Word...

Man is a sinner.

•Isaiah 53:6, "All we like sheep have gone astray; we have turned every one to his own way; and the LORD hath laid on him the iniquity of us all."

•John 3:3, "Jesus answered and said unto him, Verily, verily, I say unto thee, Except a man be born again, he cannot see the kingdom of God."

•Romans 3:10, "As it is written, There is none righteous, no, not one."

•Romans 3:23, "For all have sinned, and come short of the glory of God."

There is a price on our sin—death.

•Romans 6:23, "For the wages of sin is death; but the gift of God is eternal life through Jesus Christ our Lord."

•Romans 5:12, "Wherefore, as by one man sin entered into the world, and death by sin; and so death passed upon all men, for that all have sinned."

•2nd Thessalonians 1:8, "In flaming fire taking vengeance on them that know not God, and that obey not the gospel of our Lord Jesus Christ."

•Revelation 20:15, "And whosoever was not found written in the book of life was cast into the lake of fire."

•Revelation 21:8, "But the fearful, and unbelieving, and the abominable, and murderers, and whoremongers, and sorcerers, and idolaters, and all liars, shall have their part in the lake which burneth with fire and brimstone: which is the second death."

Jesus paid that price by dying on the cross and shedding His blood.

•Romans 5:8, "But God commendeth his love toward us, in that, while we were yet sinners, Christ died for us."

•John 3:16, "For God so loved the world, that he gave his only begotten Son, that whosoever believeth in him should not perish, but have everlasting life."

•1st Timothy 1:15, "This is a faithful saying, and worthy of all acceptation, that Christ Jesus came into the world to save sinners; of whom I am chief."

•1st Peter 1:18-19, "Forasmuch as ye know that ye were not redeemed with corruptible things, as silver and gold, from your vain conversation received by tradition from your fathers; But with the precious blood of Christ..."

By faith in Jesus Christ ALONE we can be saved.

Salvation is NOT found in a religion or good works, but in a person...the LORD JESUS CHRIST!

•John 11:25, "Jesus said unto her, I am the resurrection, and the life: he that believeth in me, though he were dead, yet shall he live:"

•John 14:6, "Jesus saith unto him, I am the way, the truth, and the life: no man cometh unto the Father, but by me."

•John 6:40, "And this is the will of him that sent me, that every one which seeth the Son, and believeth on him, may have everlasting life: and I will raise him up at the last day."

•Acts 26:18, "To open their eyes, and to turn them from darkness to light, and from the power of Satan unto God, that they may receive forgiveness of sins, and inheritance among them which are sanctified by faith that is in me."

•Romans 10:13, "For whosoever shall call upon the name of the Lord shall be saved."

•1st Corinthians 3:11, "For other foundation can no man lay than that is laid, which is Jesus Christ."

•Galatians 3:26, "For ye are all the children of God by faith in Christ Jesus."

Here is how you call upon the Lord.

Do you admit that you are a sinner under the condemnation of God?

Do you admit that you deserve Hell?

Do you believe Jesus is the Son of God (God in the flesh) who died upon the cross and shed His precious blood to pay for your sins?

If you are willing to admit your sinfulness and would like for God to save your soul, just ask Him...

Dear Jesus, I admit that I am a sinner, deserving of Hell. Please forgive me of my sins and take me to Heaven when I die. I now believe upon You alone, apart from all works and religion, as my personal Savior. Thank you. Amen.

Just as you were born physically to your parents, you were born spiritually into the Family of God when you believed on Jesus! (John 3:3).

Please understand that we are not saved because we pray a prayer; but because we believe upon the Lord Jesus Christ. It is certainly appropriate to ask the Lord in prayer to forgive and save us; but it is our faith which prompted us to pray the prayer.

You could just as easily believe in your heart upon the Lord to be saved, and not pray at all. Salvation is of the heart, as we read in Romans 10:10, "For with the heart man believeth unto righteousness..."

You do NOT have to be baptized or do anything to go to Heaven other than trust upon the Lord as your Savior ... Romans 4:5, "But to him that worketh not, but believeth on him that justifieth the ungodly, his faith is counted for righteousness."

What a wonderful Savior!

"How to go to Heaven" was arranged by by D. J. Stewart

Steps for Christian Living

1. Read and obey the Bible. Studying a few chapters here and there really adds up.

2. Pray. Talk with your best friend God.

3. Trust God. Depend on Him to give you strength and direction.

4. Share Christ with your friends.

5. Give to God and others. Money, time, love.

6. Resist Sin. "Submit yourselves therefore to God. Resist the devil, and he will flee from you"(James 4:7).

7. Gather with other Christians. Everybody needs support and encouragement.

Summary of Christian Beliefs

Genesis 1:1
In the beginning God created the heaven and the earth.

1 Timothy 3:16
Great indeed, we confess, is the mystery of our religion: He was manifested in the flesh, vindicated in the Spirit, seen by angels, preached among the nations, believed on in the world, taken up in glory.

1 Corinthians 15:3-7
For I delivered to you as of first importance what I also received, that Christ died for our sins in accordance with the scriptures, that he was buried, that he was raised on the third day in accordance with the scriptures, and that he appeared to Cephas, then to the twelve.

Revelation 22:21
The grace of our Lord Jesus Christ be with you all. Amen.

The Four Great Questions of Life

Who am I?

Where did I come from?

Why am I here?

Where am I going when I die?

You are a unique creation made in the image of God, whose purpose is to worship, obey, and be in fellowship with the loving Creator of the universe.

If you have been saved by the blood of God's only begotten Son Jesus Christ, you will live forever in paradise with God.

If you reject the only way to God, who is the source of love, peace, joy, and meaning, all that is left is an eternity filled with hatred, distress, depression, and insignificance.

The answers to the Four Great Questions are based off of the following Scriptures: Genesis 1-2; Job 42:5-6; Ecclesiastes 12:13-14; Matthew 7:13-14; Matthew 22:34-40; Mark 12:28-34; Romans 3:21-26; Revelation 19-22.

The Purpose of Life:
Be Saved by Christ

void

-adjective

1. Law. having no legal force or effect; not legally binding or enforceable.
2. useless; ineffectual; vain.
3. devoid; destitute (usually fol. by of): a life void of meaning.
4. without contents; empty.
5. without an incumbent, as an office.
6. Mathematics. (of a set) empty.
7. (in cards) having no cards in a suit.

–noun

8. an empty space; emptiness: He disappeared into the void.
9. something experienced as a loss or privation: His death left a great void in her life.
10. a gap or opening, as in a wall.
11. a vacancy; vacuum.
12. Typography. counter3 (def. 10).
13. (in cards) lack of cards in a suit: a void in clubs.

–verb (used with object)

14. to make ineffectual; invalidate; nullify: to void a check.
15. to empty; discharge; evacuate: to void excrement.
16. to clear or empty (often fol. by of): to void a chamber of occupants.
17. Archaic. to depart from; vacate.

–verb (used without object)

18. to defecate or urinate.

The First Book of Moses, Genesis

1:1 In the beginning **God** created the *heaven* and the earth.

1:2 And the **earth** was without **form**, and *void*; and *darkness* was *upon* the **face of the deep**. And the Spirit of God moved upon the face of the *waters*.

1:3 And **God** said, Let there be light: and there was **light.**

1:4 And *God* saw the light, that it was good: and God divided the light from the **darkness.**

Table of Contents for the Gospel According to Saint John

Explanatory Note

Each chapter of the Gospel of John starts with an introduction in italic script. These paragraphs are provided as a springboard for further thoughts about all the content that follows. Sometimes this beginning includes a unifying theme; other times the start provides an explanation for that which is contained after. Note that the Gospel is central to The Void, and that all the other information is intended to highlight the truth of God. The quotes from literature and other religions are only there to provide a way of seeing new insights into the framework of the Good News. In no manner are the other sources held above, or equal to, the Bible.

Chapter One, Light

"And the earth was without form, and void; and darkness was upon the face of the deep. And the Spirit of God moved upon the face of the waters. And God said, Let there be light: and there was light" *(Genesis 1:2-3). In the beginning, God filled the physical void with light; right now, God wants to fill the spiritual void in your life with Jesus Christ, the Light of the World.*

"On wheels of light, on wings of flame, The glorious hosts of Zion came."

From "The Song of Bethlehem" by Thomas Campbell.
Artist: J. R. Clayton.

∼

1:1 In the beginning was the Word, and the Word was with God, and the Word was God. 1:2 The same was in the beginning with God.
1:3 All things were made by him; and without him was not any thing made that was made. 1:4 In him was life; and the life was the light of men. 1:5 And the light shineth in darkness; and the darkness

comprehended it not. 1:6 There was a man sent from God, whose name was John. 1:7 The same came for a witness, to bear witness of the Light, that all men through him might believe. 1:8 He was not that Light, but was sent to bear witness of that Light. 1:9 That was the true Light, which lighteth every man that cometh into the world.

1:10 He was in the world, and the world was made by him, and the world knew him not. 1:11 He came unto his own, and his own received him not.

1:12 But as many as received him, to them gave he power to become the sons of God, even to them that believe on his name:

1:13 Which were born, not of blood, nor of the will of the flesh, nor of the will of man, but of God. 1:14 And the Word was made flesh, and dwelt among us, (and we beheld his glory, the glory as of the only begotten of the Father,) full of grace and truth.

1:15 John bare witness of him, and cried, saying, This was he of whom I spake, He that cometh after me is preferred before me: for he was before me. 1:16 And of his fulness have all we received, and grace for grace. 1:17 For the law was given by Moses, but grace and truth came by Jesus Christ. 1:18 No man hath seen God at any time; the only begotten Son, which is in the bosom of the Father, he hath declared him.

1:19 And this is the record of John, when the Jews sent priests and Levites from Jerusalem to ask him, Who art thou?

1:20 And he confessed, and denied not; but confessed, I am not the Christ. 1:21 And they asked him, What then? Art thou Elias? And he saith, I am not. Art thou that prophet? And he answered, No.

1:22 Then said they unto him, Who art thou? that we may give an answer to them that sent us. What sayest thou of thyself? 1:23 He said, I am the voice of one crying in the wilderness, Make straight the way of the Lord, as said the prophet Esaias. 1:24 And they which were sent were of the Pharisees.

1:25 And they asked him, and said unto him, Why baptizest thou then, if thou be not that Christ, nor Elias, neither that prophet?

1:26 John answered them, saying, I baptize with water: but there standeth one among you, whom ye know not; 1:27 He it is, who coming after me is preferred before me, whose shoe's latchet I am not worthy to unloose. 1:28 These things were done in Bethabara beyond Jordan, where John was baptizing. 1:29 The next day John seeth Jesus coming unto him, and saith, Behold the Lamb of God, which taketh away the sin of the world. 1:30 This is he of whom I said, After me cometh a man which is preferred before me: for he was before me. 1:31 And I knew him not: but that he should be made manifest to Israel, therefore am I come baptizing with water. 1:32 And John bare record, saying, I saw the Spirit descending from heaven like a dove, and it abode upon him.

1:33 And I knew him not: but he that sent me to baptize with water, the same said unto me, Upon whom thou shalt see the Spirit descending, and remaining on him, the same is he which baptizeth with the Holy Ghost. 1:34 And I saw, and bare record that this is the Son of God.

1:35 Again the next day after John stood, and two of his disciples;

1:36 And looking upon Jesus as he walked, he saith, Behold the Lamb of God! 1:37 And the two disciples heard him speak, and they followed Jesus. 1:38 Then Jesus turned, and saw them following, and saith unto them, What seek ye? They said unto him, Rabbi, (which is to say, being interpreted, Master,) where dwellest thou? 1:39 He saith unto them, Come and see. They came and saw where he dwelt, and abode with him that day: for it was about the tenth hour. 1:40 One of the two which heard John speak, and followed him, was Andrew, Simon Peter's brother. 1:41 He first findeth his own brother Simon, and saith unto him, We have found the Messias, which is, being interpreted, the Christ. 1:42 And he brought him to Jesus. And when Jesus beheld him, he said, Thou art Simon the son of Jona: thou shalt be called Cephas, which is by interpretation, A stone. 1:43 The day following Jesus would go forth into Galilee, and findeth Philip, and saith unto him, Follow me.

1:44 Now Philip was of Bethsaida, the city of Andrew and Peter.

1:45 Philip findeth Nathanael, and saith unto him, We have found him, of whom Moses in the law, and the prophets, did write, Jesus of Nazareth, the son of Joseph. 1:46 And Nathanael said unto him, Can there any good thing come out of Nazareth? Philip saith unto him, Come and see. 1:47 Jesus saw Nathanael coming to him, and saith of him, Behold an Israelite indeed, in whom is no guile!

1:48 Nathanael saith unto him, Whence knowest thou me? Jesus answered and said unto him, Before that Philip called thee, when thou wast under the fig tree, I saw thee. 1:49 Nathanael answered and saith unto him, Rabbi, thou art the Son of God; thou art the King of Israel. 1:50 Jesus answered and said unto him, Because I said unto thee, I saw thee under the fig tree, believest thou? Thou shalt see greater things than these. 1:51 And he saith unto him, Verily, verily, I say unto you, Hereafter ye shall see heaven open, and the angels of God ascending and descending upon the Son of man.

Is there a void in your life?

_____
_____
_____
_____
_____
_____
_____

Book One from *The Confessions of Saint Augustine* by Saint Augustine

Great art Thou, O Lord, and greatly to be praised; great is Thy power, and Thy wisdom infinite. And Thee would man praise; man, but a particle of Thy creation; man, that bears about him his mortality, the witness of his sin, the witness that Thou resistest the proud: yet would man praise Thee; he, but a particle of Thy creation.

Two Cherubs on a Book
Source: William Blades: "Pentateuch of Printing with a Chapter on Judges"

103

Memorization: Filling the Void with God's Word

A unique feature of The Void is including the chapter number in the text along with the verse. This allows for the reader to make a mental picture of the whole verse along with the necessary reference numbers. Other Bibles only have a chapter heading with verse numbering. This distance from chapter to verse can increase memorizing difficulty.

Tips for Memorization

Summarize the meaning of the verse in your own words.

Read the verse aloud.

Close your eyes and picture the words of the verse in your mind.

Say the verse aloud with your eyes closed.

Write the verse on a blank sheet of paper.

Review the verse throughout the day.

Break the verse into smaller pieces.

If possible, give motions to the verse. For example: John 2:15

Move your hands as if you were overturning tables.

Draw a picture of the verse. For example: John 2:3

Draw grapes and a cup and then put an x through them.

Read Psalm 119 to discover how important God's Law was to King David.

119: 97 "O how love I thy law! it is my meditation all the day."

Chapter Two, Hunger

There are different types of hunger. Some crave for knowledge, others thirst for wine, and others desire wealth. Most people seek the temporary taste; few yearn for the delight of the eternal. Book smarts are ephemeral, but "The fear of the LORD is the beginning of wisdom: and the knowledge of the holy is understanding"(Proverbs 9:10). The tongue will never be satisfied with drink, "But whosoever drinketh of the water that I shall give him shall never thirst; but the water that I shall give him shall be in him a well of water springing up into everlasting life"(John 4:14). The value of money is finite so "lay up for yourselves treasures in heaven, where neither moth nor rust doth corrupt, and where thieves do not break through nor steal"(Matthew 6:20).

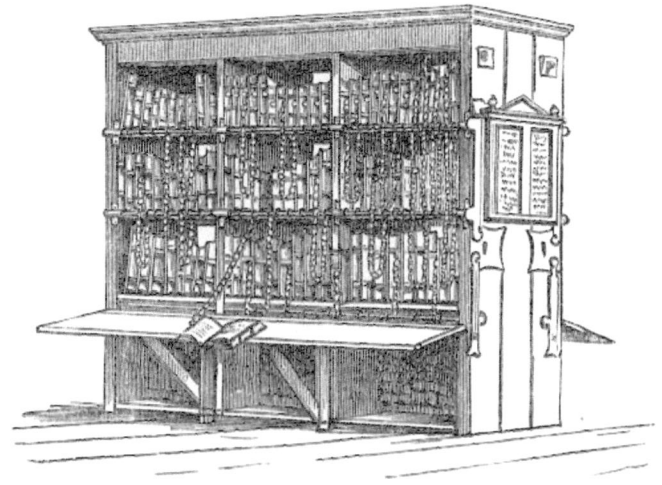

Books Attached to Shelf by Chain
Source: William Andrews: "Curiosities of the Church: Studies of Curious Customs, Services and Records"

～

2:1 And the third day there was a marriage in Cana of Galilee; and the mother of Jesus was there: 2:2 And both Jesus was called, and his disciples, to the marriage. 2:3 And when they wanted wine, the mother of Jesus saith unto him, They have no wine.

2:4 Jesus saith unto her, Woman, what have I to do with thee? mine hour is not yet come. 2:5 His mother saith unto the servants, Whatsoever he saith unto you, do it. 2:6 And there were set there six waterpots of stone, after the manner of the purifying of the Jews, containing two or three firkins apiece. 2:7 Jesus saith unto them, Fill the waterpots with water. And they filled them up to the brim.

2:8 And he saith unto them, Draw out now, and bear unto the governor of the feast. And they bare it. 2:9 When the ruler of the feast had tasted the water that was made wine, and knew not whence it was: (but the servants which drew the water knew;) the governor of the feast called the bridegroom, 2:10 And saith unto him, Every man at the beginning doth set forth good wine; and when men have well drunk, then that which is worse: but thou hast kept the good wine until now.

2:11 This beginning of miracles did Jesus in Cana of Galilee, and manifested forth his glory; and his disciples believed on him.

2:12 After this he went down to Capernaum, he, and his mother, and his brethren, and his disciples: and they continued there not many days. 2:13 And the Jews' passover was at hand, and Jesus went up to Jerusalem, 2:14 And found in the temple those that sold oxen and sheep and doves, and the changers of money sitting: 2:15 And when he had made a scourge of small cords, he drove them all out of the temple, and the sheep, and the oxen; and poured out the changers' money, and overthrew the tables; 2:16 And said unto them that sold doves, Take these things hence; make not my Father's house an house of merchandise. 2:17 And his disciples remembered that it was written, The zeal of thine house hath eaten me up.

2:18 Then answered the Jews and said unto him, What sign shewest thou unto us, seeing that thou doest these things?

2:19 Jesus answered and said unto them, Destroy this temple, and in three days I will raise it up. 2:20 Then said the Jews, Forty and six years was this temple in building, and wilt thou rear it up in three days?

2:21 But he spake of the temple of his body.

2:22 When therefore he was risen from the dead, his disciples remembered that he had said this unto them; and they believed the scripture, and the word which Jesus had said. 2:23 Now when he was in Jerusalem at the passover, in the feast day, many believed in his name, when they saw the miracles which he did. 2:24 But Jesus did not commit himself unto them, because he knew all men, 2:25 And needed not that any should testify of man: for he knew what was in man.

Do you hunger for a miracle in your life?

_____
_____
_____
_____
_____
_____
_____

The Preface from *A Treatise Concerning the Principles of Human Knowledge*
by George Berkeley

What I here make public has, after a long and scrupulous inquiry, seemed to me evidently true and not unuseful to be known-particularly to those who are tainted with Scepticism, or want a demonstration of the existence and immateriality of God, or the natural immortality of the soul. Whether it be so or no I am content the reader should impartially examine; since I do not think myself any farther concerned for the success of what I have written than as it is agreeable to truth. But, to the end this may not suffer, I make it my request that the reader suspend his judgment till he has once at least read the whole through with that degree of attention and thought which the subject-matter shall seem to deserve.

Children with their Teacher
Source: Anonymous: "Chatterbox Annual"

Chapter Three, Spirit

"And the LORD God formed man of the dust of the ground, and breathed into his nostrils the breath of life; and man became a living soul"(Genesis 2:7). Just as man was created with the Spirit of God, so must man be recreated by the Holy Spirit. After the Fall, man became spiritually dead; thus man must be spiritually reborn. In contrast to the fictitious fairy Ariel, or the story of When Lion Could Fly (see below), the spiritual rebirth is as real as physical birth. Jesus is emphatic that man must be born again before he can enter the Kingdom of God (John 3:5).

Ariel
Source: William Shakespeare: "The Works of Shakspere, with notes by Charles Knight"

~

3:1 There was a man of the Pharisees, named Nicodemus, a ruler of the Jews: 3:2 The same came to Jesus by night, and said unto him, Rabbi, we know that thou art a teacher come from God: for no man can do these miracles that thou doest, except God be with him.
3:3 Jesus answered and said unto him, Verily, verily, I say unto thee, Except a man be born again, he cannot see the kingdom of God.
3:4 Nicodemus saith unto him, How can a man be born when he is old? can he enter the second time into his mother's womb, and be born?
3:5 Jesus answered, Verily, verily, I say unto thee, Except a man be born

of water and of the Spirit, he cannot enter into the kingdom of God.

3:6 That which is born of the flesh is flesh; and that which is born of the Spirit is spirit.

3:7 Marvel not that I said unto thee, Ye must be born again.

3:8 The wind bloweth where it listeth, and thou hearest the sound thereof, but canst not tell whence it cometh, and whither it goeth: so is every one that is born of the Spirit. 3:9 Nicodemus answered and said unto him, How can these things be? 3:10 Jesus answered and said unto him, Art thou a master of Israel, and knowest not these things?

3:11 Verily, verily, I say unto thee, We speak that we do know, and testify that we have seen; and ye receive not our witness. 3:12 If I have told you earthly things, and ye believe not, how shall ye believe, if I tell you of heavenly things?

3:13 And no man hath ascended up to heaven, but he that came down from heaven, even the Son of man which is in heaven.

3:14 And as Moses lifted up the serpent in the wilderness, even so must the Son of man be lifted up: 3:15 That whosoever believeth in him should not perish, but have eternal life. 3:16 For God so loved the world, that he gave his only begotten Son, that whosoever believeth in him should not perish, but have everlasting life. 3:17 For God sent not his Son into the world to condemn the world; but that the world through him might be saved. 3:18 He that believeth on him is not condemned: but he that believeth not is condemned already, because he hath not believed in the name of the only begotten Son of God. 3:19 And this is the condemnation, that light is come into the world, and men loved darkness rather than light, because their deeds were evil.

3:20 For every one that doeth evil hateth the light, neither cometh to the light, lest his deeds should be reproved. 3:21 But he that doeth truth cometh to the light, that his deeds may be made manifest, that they are wrought in God. 3:22 After these things came Jesus and his disciples into the land of Judaea; and there he tarried with them, and baptized. 3:23 And John also was baptizing in Aenon near to Salim, because there was much water there: and they came, and were baptized.

3:24 For John was not yet cast into prison. 3:25 Then there arose a question between some of John's disciples and the Jews about purifying. 3:26 And they came unto John, and said unto him, Rabbi, he that was with thee beyond Jordan, to whom thou barest witness, behold, the same baptizeth, and all men come to him. 3:27 John answered and said, A man can receive nothing, except it be given him from heaven.

3:28 Ye yourselves bear me witness, that I said, I am not the Christ, but that I am sent before him. 3:29 He that hath the bride is the bridegroom: but the friend of the bridegroom, which standeth and heareth him, rejoiceth greatly because of the bridegroom's voice: this my joy therefore is fulfilled.

3:30 He must increase, but I must decrease. 3:31 He that cometh from above is above all: he that is of the earth is earthly, and speaketh of the earth: he that cometh from heaven is above all. 3:32 And what he hath seen and heard, that he testifieth; and no man receiveth his testimony. 3:33 He that hath received his testimony hath set to his seal that God is true. 3:34 For he whom God hath sent speaketh the words of God: for God giveth not the Spirit by measure unto him. 3:35 The Father loveth the Son, and hath given all things into his hand. 3:36 He that believeth on the Son hath everlasting life: and he that believeth not the Son shall not see life; but the wrath of God abideth on him.

Have you been born of water and of the Spirit? Why?

_____
_____
_____
_____
_____
_____
_____

When Lion Could Fly from *South African Folk-Tales* by James A. Honey

Lion, it is said, used once to fly, and at that time nothing could live before him. As he was unwilling that the bones of what he caught should be broken into pieces, he made a pair of White Crows watch the bones, leaving them behind at the kraal whilst he went a-hunting. But one day Great Frog came there, broke the bones in pieces, and said, "Why can men and animals live no longer?" And he added these words, "When he comes, tell him that I live at yonder pool; if he wishes to see me, he must come there."

Lion, lying in wait (for game), wanted to fly up, but found he could not fly. Then he got angry, thinking that at the kraal something was wrong, and returned home. When he arrived, he asked, "What have you done that I cannot fly?" Then they answered and said, "Some one came here, broke the bones into pieces, and said, 'If he want me, he may look for me at yonder pool!'"

Lion went, and arrived while Frog was sitting at the water's edge, and he tried to creep stealthily upon him. When he was about to get hold of him, Frog said, "Ho!" and, diving, went to the other side of the pool, and sat there. Lion pursued him; but as he could not catch him he returned home.

From that day, it is said, Lion walked on his feet, and also began to creep upon (his game); and the White Crows became entirely dumb since the day that they said, "Nothing can be said of that matter."

Samsaraand Nirvana from *Buddha, The Gospel* by Paul Carus

Look about and contemplate life! Everything is transient and nothing endures. There is birth and death, growth and decay; there is combination and separation. The glory of the world is like a flower: it stands in full bloom in the morning and fades in the heat of the day.

The monogram IHS comes from the Greek for Jesus, IHESUS, or from the Latin Ihesus Hominum Salvator, which is, Jesus, Saviour of Mankind.
Source: F. Delamotte: "Ornamental Alphabets, Ancient and Mediæval"

Chapter Four, Rest

All humans require rest; sometimes relaxation fulfills this need, other times sleep is necessary. Nobody can get around this necessity. Even Jesus was wearied and sat down by a well to revive his body by taking a break. As Leonardo Da Vinci points out below, shadow is a partner to light, in the same manner that sleep is a couple with consciousness. These concepts must remain in harmony, otherwise chaos results. Sleep is difficult in a bright environment; the absence of light hampers normal activities.

This is a "half-tester" bed, that is, with a canopy but without supporting posts at the feet.
Source: Charles Knight: "Old England: A Pictorial Museum"

~

4:1 When therefore the Lord knew how the Pharisees had heard that Jesus made and baptized more disciples than John,
4:2 (Though Jesus himself baptized not, but his disciples,)
4:3 He left Judaea, and departed again into Galilee.
4:4 And he must needs go through Samaria. 4:5 Then cometh he to a city of Samaria, which is called Sychar, near to the parcel of ground that Jacob gave to his son Joseph. 4:6 Now Jacob's well was there. Jesus therefore, being wearied with his journey, sat thus on the well: and it

was about the sixth hour.

4:7 There cometh a woman of Samaria to draw water: Jesus saith unto her, Give me to drink. 4:8 (For his disciples were gone away unto the city to buy meat.) 4:9 Then saith the woman of Samaria unto him, How is it that thou, being a Jew, askest drink of me, which am a woman of Samaria? for the Jews have no dealings with the Samaritans.

4:10 Jesus answered and said unto her, If thou knewest the gift of God, and who it is that saith to thee, Give me to drink; thou wouldest have asked of him, and he would have given thee living water.

4:11 The woman saith unto him, Sir, thou hast nothing to draw with, and the well is deep: from whence then hast thou that living water?

4:12 Art thou greater than our father Jacob, which gave us the well, and drank thereof himself, and his children, and his cattle?

4:13 Jesus answered and said unto her, Whosoever drinketh of this water shall thirst again:

4:14 But whosoever drinketh of the water that I shall give him shall never thirst; but the water that I shall give him shall be in him a well of water springing up into everlasting life.

4:15 The woman saith unto him, Sir, give me this water, that I thirst not, neither come hither to draw. 4:16 Jesus saith unto her, Go, call thy husband, and come hither. 4:17 The woman answered and said, I have no husband. Jesus said unto her, Thou hast well said, I have no husband: 4:18 For thou hast had five husbands; and he whom thou now hast is not thy husband: in that saidst thou truly. 4:19 The woman saith unto him, Sir, I perceive that thou art a prophet. 4:20 Our fathers worshipped in this mountain; and ye say, that in Jerusalem is the place where men ought to worship. 4:21 Jesus saith unto her, Woman, believe me, the hour cometh, when ye shall neither in this mountain, nor yet at Jerusalem, worship the Father. 4:22 Ye worship ye know not what: we know what we worship: for salvation is of the Jews. 4:23 But the hour cometh, and now is, when the true worshippers shall worship the Father in spirit and in truth: for the Father seeketh such to worship him.

4:24 God is a Spirit: and they that worship him must worship him in spirit and in truth. 4:25 The woman saith unto him, I know that Messias cometh, which is called Christ: when he is come, he will tell us all things. 4:26 Jesus saith unto her, I that speak unto thee am he.

4:27 And upon this came his disciples, and marvelled that he talked with the woman: yet no man said, What seekest thou? Or, Why talkest thou with her? 4:28 The woman then left her waterpot, and went her way into the city, and saith to the men, 4:29 Come, see a man, which told me all things that ever I did: is not this the Christ?

4:30 Then they went out of the city, and came unto him.

4:31 In the mean while his disciples prayed him, saying, Master, eat.

4:32 But he said unto them, I have meat to eat that ye know not of.

4:33 Therefore said the disciples one to another, Hath any man brought him ought to eat? 4:34 Jesus saith unto them, My meat is to do the will of him that sent me, and to finish his work. 4:35 Say not ye, There are yet four months, and then cometh harvest? behold, I say unto you, Lift up your eyes, and look on the fields; for they are white already to harvest. 4:36 And he that reapeth receiveth wages, and gathereth fruit unto life eternal: that both he that soweth and he that reapeth may rejoice together. 4:37 And herein is that saying true, One soweth, and another reapeth. 4:38 I sent you to reap that whereon ye bestowed no labour: other men laboured, and ye are entered into their labours.

4:39 And many of the Samaritans of that city believed on him for the saying of the woman, which testified, He told me all that ever I did. 4:40 So when the Samaritans were come unto him, they besought him that he would tarry with them: and he abode there two days.

4:41 And many more believed because of his own word;

4:42 And said unto the woman, Now we believe, not because of thy saying: for we have heard him ourselves, and know that this is indeed the Christ, the Saviour of the world.

4:43 Now after two days he departed thence, and went into Galilee. 4:44 For Jesus himself testified, that a prophet hath no honour in his own country. 4:45 Then when he was come into Galilee, the Galilaeans received him, having seen all the things that he did at Jerusalem at the feast: for they also went unto the feast. 4:46 So Jesus came again into Cana of Galilee, where he made the water wine. And there was a certain nobleman, whose son was sick at Capernaum. 4:47 When he heard that Jesus was come out of Judaea into Galilee, he went unto him, and besought him that he would come down, and heal his son: for he was at the point of death. 4:48 Then said Jesus unto him, Except ye see signs and wonders, ye will not believe. 4:49 The nobleman saith unto him, Sir, come down ere my child die. 4:50 Jesus saith unto him, Go thy way; thy son liveth. And the man believed the word that Jesus had spoken unto him, and he went his way. 4:51 And as he was now going down, his servants met him, and told him, saying, Thy son liveth.

4:52 Then enquired he of them the hour when he began to amend. And they said unto him, Yesterday at the seventh hour the fever left him. 4:53 So the father knew that it was at the same hour, in the which Jesus said unto him, Thy son liveth: and himself believed, and his whole house. 4:54 This is again the second miracle that Jesus did, when he was come out of Judaea into Galilee.

What does the water pot the woman left by the well represent?

_____
_____
_____
_____
_____
_____
_____

From the Introduction of Six Books on Light and Shade
from *The Notebooks of Leonardo Da Vinci*
by Jean Paul Richter

Shadow is the obstruction of light. Shadows appear to me to be of supreme importance in perspective, because, without them opaque and solid bodies will be ill defined; that which is contained within their outlines and their boundaries themselves will be ill-understood unless they are shown against a background of a different tone from themselves. And therefore in my first proposition concerning shadow I state that every opaque body is surrounded and its whole surface enveloped in shadow and light. And on this proposition I build up the first Book.

Vernal Equinox
Source: William Hone: "Hone's Everyday Book"

Chapter Five, Work

There are different manners of work. You can brush your bristles, move your mat, survive in life, or think deep thoughts. No matter the task, our work should be for the glory of God. Personal hygiene helps provide a proper platform for the presentation of the Gospel. Heavy lifting can be done to honor the strength that God has provided to humankind. Struggling through life can be an act of trusting in God, and when you think deeply you can "be ye transformed by the renewing of your mind, that ye may prove what is that good, and acceptable, and perfect, will of God"(Romans 12:2).

Lobster primping before a mirror
Source: Lewis Caroll: "Alice's Adventures in Wonderland"
Artist: Sir John Tenniel
Engraver: Dalziel

~

5:1 After this there was a feast of the Jews; and Jesus went up to Jerusalem. 5:2 Now there is at Jerusalem by the sheep market a pool, which is called in the Hebrew tongue Bethesda, having five porches. 5:3 In these lay a great multitude of impotent folk, of blind, halt, withered, waiting for the moving of the water. 5:4 For an angel went down at a certain season into the pool, and troubled the water: whosoever then first after the troubling of the water stepped in was made whole of whatsoever disease he had. 5:5 And a certain man was there, which had an infirmity thirty and eight years. 5:6 When Jesus saw him lie, and knew that he had been now a long time in that case, he saith unto him, Wilt thou be made whole? 5:7 The impotent man answered him, Sir, I have no man, when the water is troubled, to put me into the pool: but while I am coming, another steppeth down before me. 5:8 Jesus saith unto him, Rise, take up thy bed, and walk.

5:9 And immediately the man was made whole, and took up his bed, and walked: and on the same day was the sabbath.

5:10 The Jews therefore said unto him that was cured, It is the sabbath day: it is not lawful for thee to carry thy bed. 5:11 He answered them, He that made me whole, the same said unto me, Take up thy bed, and walk.

5:12 Then asked they him, What man is that which said unto thee, Take up thy bed, and walk? 5:13 And he that was healed wist not who it was: for Jesus had conveyed himself away, a multitude being in that place. 5:14 Afterward Jesus findeth him in the temple, and said unto him, Behold, thou art made whole: sin no more, lest a worse thing come unto thee. 5:15 The man departed, and told the Jews that it was Jesus, which had made him whole. 5:16 And therefore did the Jews persecute Jesus, and sought to slay him, because he had done these things on the sabbath day. 5:17 But Jesus answered them, My Father worketh hitherto, and I work. 5:18 Therefore the Jews sought the more to kill him, because he not only had broken the sabbath, but said also that God was his Father, making himself equal with God.

5:19 Then answered Jesus and said unto them, Verily, verily, I say unto you, The Son can do nothing of himself, but what he seeth the Father do: for what things soever he doeth, these also doeth the Son likewise. 5:20 For the Father loveth the Son, and sheweth him all things that himself doeth: and he will shew him greater works than these, that ye may marvel. 5:21 For as the Father raiseth up the dead, and quickeneth them; even so the Son quickeneth whom he will. 5:22 For the Father judgeth no man, but hath committed all judgment unto the Son:

5:23 That all men should honour the Son, even as they honour the Father. He that honoureth not the Son honoureth not the Father which hath sent him. 5:24 Verily, verily, I say unto you, He that heareth my word, and believeth on him that sent me, hath everlasting life, and shall not come into condemnation; but is passed from death unto life.

5:25 Verily, verily, I say unto you, The hour is coming, and now is, when the dead shall hear the voice of the Son of God: and they that hear shall live. 5:26 For as the Father hath life in himself; so hath he given to the Son to have life in himself; 5:27 And hath given him authority to execute judgment also, because he is the Son of man.

5:28 Marvel not at this: for the hour is coming, in the which all that are in the graves shall hear his voice, 5:29 And shall come forth; they that have done good, unto the resurrection of life; and they that have done evil, unto the resurrection of damnation. 5:30 I can of mine own self do nothing: as I hear, I judge: and my judgment is just; because I seek not mine own will, but the will of the Father which hath sent me.

5:31 If I bear witness of myself, my witness is not true.

5:32 There is another that beareth witness of me; and I know that the witness which he witnesseth of me is true. 5:33 Ye sent unto John, and he bare witness unto the truth. 5:34 But I receive not testimony from man: but these things I say, that ye might be saved. 5:35 He was a burning and a shining light: and ye were willing for a season to rejoice in his light. 5:36 But I have greater witness than that of John: for the works which the Father hath given me to finish, the same works that I do, bear witness of me, that the Father hath sent me.

5:37 And the Father himself, which hath sent me, hath borne witness of me. Ye have neither heard his voice at any time, nor seen his shape. 5:38 And ye have not his word abiding in you: for whom he hath sent, him ye believe not. 5:39 Search the scriptures; for in them ye think ye have eternal life: and they are they which testify of me.

5:40 And ye will not come to me, that ye might have life.

5:41 I receive not honour from men. 5:42 But I know you, that ye have not the love of God in you. 5:43 I am come in my Father's name, and ye receive me not: if another shall come in his own name, him ye will receive. 5:44 How can ye believe, which receive honour one of another, and seek not the honour that cometh from God only? 5:45 Do not think that I will accuse you to the Father: there is one that accuseth you, even Moses, in whom ye trust. 5:46 For had ye believed Moses, ye would have believed me: for he wrote of me. 5:47 But if ye believe not his writings, how shall ye believe my words?

How do you work for the Lord?

_____

_____

_____

_____

_____

_____

_____

Difficulties of the Theory from *On the Origin of Species by Means of Natural Selection, or the Preservation of Favoured Races in the Struggle for Life*
by Charles Darwin

Long before the reader has arrived at this part of my work, a crowd of difficulties will have occurred to him. Some of them are so serious that to this day I can hardly reflect on them without being in some degree staggered; but, to the best of my judgment, the greater number are only apparent, and those that are real are not, I think, fatal to the theory.

These difficulties and objections may be classed under the following heads: First, why, if species have descended from other species by fine gradations, do we not everywhere see innumerable transitional forms? Why is not all nature in confusion, instead of the species being, as we see them, well defined?

Part One from *Discourse on the Method of Rightly Conducting the Reason and Seeking Truth in the Sciences*
by Rene Descartes

Good sense is, of all things among men, the most equally distributed; for every one thinks himself so abundantly provided with it, that those even who are the most difficult to satisfy in everything else, do not usually desire a larger measure of this quality than they already possess.

And in this it is not likely that all are mistaken the conviction is rather to be held as testifying that the power of judging aright and of distinguishing truth from error, which is properly what is called good sense or reason, is by nature equal in all men; and that the diversity of our opinions, consequently, does not arise from some being endowed with a larger share of reason than others, but solely from this, that we conduct our thoughts along different ways, and do not fix our attention on the same objects. For to be possessed of a vigorous mind is not enough; the prime requisite is rightly to apply it. The greatest minds, as they are capable of the highest excellences, are open likewise to the greatest aberrations; and those who travel very slowly may yet make far greater progress, provided they keep always to the straight road, than those who, while they run, forsake it.

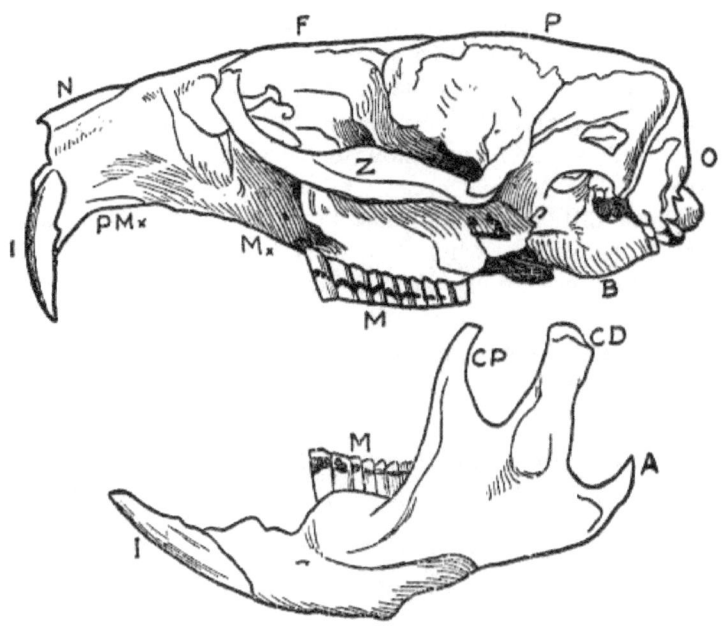

Skull & One Side of Mandible of Musk Rat.
Source: Stone, William and Cram, William Everett: "American Animals"

Chapter Six, Thinking

Our thoughts are important to God. David realized that God knew what he was thinking. He said, "Thou knowest my downsitting and mine uprising, thou understandest my thought afar off"(Psalm 139:2). We should keep our minds clean. Whether we are playing a game, eating a meal, or thinking about philosophy, our minds should be focused on "whatsoever things are true, whatsoever things are honest, whatsoever things are just, whatsoever things are pure, whatsoever things are lovely, whatsoever things are of good report"(Phillipians 4:8).

Lady and Youth Playing Draughts,
Source: J. R. Green: "A Short History of the English People"

~

6:1 After these things Jesus went over the sea of Galilee, which is the sea of Tiberias. 6:2 And a great multitude followed him, because they saw his miracles which he did on them that were diseased.
6:3 And Jesus went up into a mountain, and there he sat with his disciples. 6:4 And the passover, a feast of the Jews, was nigh.
6:5 When Jesus then lifted up his eyes, and saw a great company come unto him, he saith unto Philip, Whence shall we buy bread, that these may eat? 6:6 And this he said to prove him: for he himself knew what

he would do. 6:7 Philip answered him, Two hundred pennyworth of bread is not sufficient for them, that every one of them may take a little. 6:8 One of his disciples, Andrew, Simon Peter's brother, saith unto him, 6:9 There is a lad here, which hath five barley loaves, and two small fishes: but what are they among so many? 6:10 And Jesus said, Make the men sit down. Now there was much grass in the place. So the men sat down, in number about five thousand. 6:11 And Jesus took the loaves; and when he had given thanks, he distributed to the disciples, and the disciples to them that were set down; and likewise of the fishes as much as they would. 6:12 When they were filled, he said unto his disciples, Gather up the fragments that remain, that nothing be lost.

6:13 Therefore they gathered them together, and filled twelve baskets with the fragments of the five barley loaves, which remained over and above unto them that had eaten. 6:14 Then those men, when they had seen the miracle that Jesus did, said, This is of a truth that prophet that should come into the world. 6:15 When Jesus therefore perceived that they would come and take him by force, to make him a king, he departed again into a mountain himself alone. 6:16 And when even was now come, his disciples went down unto the sea, 6:17 And entered into a ship, and went over the sea toward Capernaum. And it was now dark, and Jesus was not come to them. 6:18 And the sea arose by reason of a great wind that blew. 6:19 So when they had rowed about five and twenty or thirty furlongs, they see Jesus walking on the sea, and drawing nigh unto the ship: and they were afraid. 6:20 But he saith unto them, It is I; be not afraid. 6:21 Then they willingly received him into the ship: and immediately the ship was at the land whither they went.

6:22 The day following, when the people which stood on the other side of the sea saw that there was none other boat there, save that one whereinto his disciples were entered, and that Jesus went not with his disciples into the boat, but that his disciples were gone away alone;

6:23 (Howbeit there came other boats from Tiberias nigh unto the place where they did eat bread, after that the Lord had given thanks:)

6:24 When the people therefore saw that Jesus was not there, neither his disciples, they also took shipping, and came to Capernaum, seeking for Jesus.

6:25 And when they had found him on the other side of the sea, they said unto him, Rabbi, when camest thou hither?

6:26 Jesus answered them and said, Verily, verily, I say unto you, Ye seek me, not because ye saw the miracles, but because ye did eat of the loaves, and were filled. 6:27 Labour not for the meat which perisheth, but for that meat which endureth unto everlasting life, which the Son of man shall give unto you: for him hath God the Father sealed.

6:28 Then said they unto him, What shall we do, that we might work the works of God? 6:29 Jesus answered and said unto them, This is the work of God, that ye believe on him whom he hath sent.

6:30 They said therefore unto him, What sign shewest thou then, that we may see, and believe thee? what dost thou work?

6:31 Our fathers did eat manna in the desert; as it is written, He gave them bread from heaven to eat. 6:32 Then Jesus said unto them, Verily, verily, I say unto you, Moses gave you not that bread from heaven; but my Father giveth you the true bread from heaven. 6:33 For the bread of God is he which cometh down from heaven, and giveth life unto the world. 6:34 Then said they unto him, Lord, evermore give us this bread. 6:35 And Jesus said unto them, I am the bread of life: he that cometh to me shall never hunger; and he that believeth on me shall never thirst. 6:36 But I said unto you, That ye also have seen me, and believe not. 6:37 All that the Father giveth me shall come to me; and him that cometh to me I will in no wise cast out. 6:38 For I came down from heaven, not to do mine own will, but the will of him that sent me.

6:39 And this is the Father's will which hath sent me, that of all which he hath given me I should lose nothing, but should raise it up again at the last day. 6:40 And this is the will of him that sent me, that every one which seeth the Son, and believeth on him, may have everlasting life: and I will raise him up at the last day. 6:41 The Jews then murmured at him, because he said, I am the bread which came down from heaven. 6:42 And they said, Is not this Jesus, the son of Joseph, whose father and mother we know? how is it then that he saith, I came down from heaven? 6:43 Jesus therefore answered and said unto them, Murmur not among yourselves. 6:44 No man can come to me, except the Father which hath sent me draw him: and I will raise him up at the last day. 6:45 It is written in the prophets, And they shall be all taught of God. Every man therefore that hath heard, and hath learned of the Father, cometh unto me. 6:46 Not that any man hath seen the Father, save he which is of God, he hath seen the Father.

6:47 Verily, verily, I say unto you, He that believeth on me hath everlasting life. 6:48 I am that bread of life. 6:49 Your fathers did eat manna in the wilderness, and are dead. 6:50 This is the bread which cometh down from heaven, that a man may eat thereof, and not die.

6:51 I am the living bread which came down from heaven: if any man eat of this bread, he shall live for ever: and the bread that I will give is my flesh, which I will give for the life of the world.

6:52 The Jews therefore strove among themselves, saying, How can this man give us his flesh to eat?

6:53 Then Jesus said unto them, Verily, verily, I say unto you, Except ye eat the flesh of the Son of man, and drink his blood, ye have no life in you. 6:54 Whoso eateth my flesh, and drinketh my blood, hath eternal life; and I will raise him up at the last day. 6:55 For my flesh is meat indeed, and my blood is drink indeed. 6:56 He that eateth my flesh, and drinketh my blood, dwelleth in me, and I in him. 6:57 As the living Father hath sent me, and I live by the Father: so he that eateth me, even he shall live by me. 6:58 This is that bread which came down from heaven: not as your fathers did eat manna, and are dead: he that eateth of this bread shall live for ever. 6:59 These things said he in the synagogue, as he taught in Capernaum. 6:60 Many therefore of his disciples, when they had heard this, said, This is an hard saying; who can hear it? 6:61 When Jesus knew in himself that his disciples murmured at it, he said unto them, Doth this offend you?

6:62 What and if ye shall see the Son of man ascend up where he was before?

6:63 It is the spirit that quickeneth; the flesh profiteth nothing: the words that I speak unto you, they are spirit, and they are life.

6:64 But there are some of you that believe not. For Jesus knew from the beginning who they were that believed not, and who should betray him. 6:65 And he said, Therefore said I unto you, that no man can come unto me, except it were given unto him of my Father.

6:66 From that time many of his disciples went back, and walked no more with him.

6:67 Then said Jesus unto the twelve, Will ye also go away?

6:68 Then Simon Peter answered him, Lord, to whom shall we go? thou hast the words of eternal life. 6:69 And we believe and are sure that thou art that Christ, the Son of the living God.

6:70 Jesus answered them, Have not I chosen you twelve, and one of you is a devil? 6:71 He spake of Judas Iscariot the son of Simon: for he it was that should betray him, being one of the twelve.

What do you spend your time thinking about?

_____
_____
_____
_____
_____
_____
_____

Why I Am An Agnostic
by Clarence Darrow

An agnostic is a doubter. The word is generally applied to those who doubt the verity of accepted religious creeds of faiths. Everyone is an agnostic as to the beliefs or creeds they do not accept. Catholics are agnostic to the Protestant creeds, and the Protestants are agnostic to the Catholic creed. Any one who thinks is an agnostic about something, otherwise he must believe that he is possessed of all knowledge. And the proper place for such a person is in the madhouse or the home for the feeble-minded. In a popular way, in the western world, an agnostic is one who doubts or disbelieves the main tenets of the Christian faith.

The Transcendentalist
by Ralph Waldo Emerson

As thinkers, mankind have ever divided into two sects, Materialists and Idealists; the first class founding on experience, the second on consciousness; the first class beginning to think from the data of the senses, the second class perceive that the senses are not final, and say, the senses give us representations of things, but what are the things themselves, they cannot tell. The materialist insists on facts, on history, on the force of circumstances, and the animal wants of man; the idealist on the power of Thought and of Will, on inspiration, on miracle, on individual culture.

?

Chapter Seven, Music

Music is a language beyond all other languages. For music is able to penetrate past the intellect to the soul; once in the soul, music has the ability to affect the innermost being of a person. There is a part of humans that is deeper than the brain's ability to understand music. For the musically inclined part of the brain does not tell one whether or not to listen to music, or what the meaning behind the music is. There is a psyche inside the person that is touched by the sounds in a way the musical faculty is not. Music reverberates with the soul. In the same manner as music, Jesus' words mold the heart. Although joyous music has little effect on someone grieving over a death, the comfort of the Lord can overcome any manner of pain.

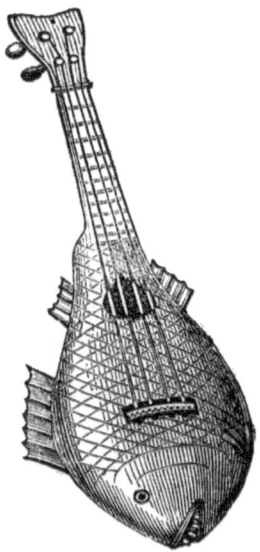

Musical Instruments at the South Kensington Museum: D.—Machête.
Source: George C. Leighton: "Illustrated London News Vol 56"

~

7:1 After these things Jesus walked in Galilee: for he would not walk in Jewry, because the Jews sought to kill him.
7:2 Now the Jews' feast of tabernacles was at hand.

7:3 His brethren therefore said unto him, Depart hence, and go into Judaea, that thy disciples also may see the works that thou doest.

7:4 For there is no man that doeth any thing in secret, and he himself seeketh to be known openly. If thou do these things, shew thyself to the world. 7:5 For neither did his brethren believe in him.

7:6 Then Jesus said unto them, My time is not yet come: but your time is always ready. 7:7 The world cannot hate you; but me it hateth, because I testify of it, that the works thereof are evil. 7:8 Go ye up unto this feast: I go not up yet unto this feast; for my time is not yet full come. 7:9 When he had said these words unto them, he abode still in Galilee. 7:10 But when his brethren were gone up, then went he also up unto the feast, not openly, but as it were in secret. 7:11 Then the Jews sought him at the feast, and said, Where is he? 7:12 And there was much murmuring among the people concerning him: for some said, He is a good man: others said, Nay; but he deceiveth the people.

7:13 Howbeit no man spake openly of him for fear of the Jews.

7:14 Now about the midst of the feast Jesus went up into the temple, and taught. 7:15 And the Jews marvelled, saying, How knoweth this man letters, having never learned? 7:16 Jesus answered them, and said, My doctrine is not mine, but his that sent me. 7:17 If any man will do his will, he shall know of the doctrine, whether it be of God, or whether I speak of myself. 7:18 He that speaketh of himself seeketh his own glory: but he that seeketh his glory that sent him, the same is true, and no unrighteousness is in him. 7:19 Did not Moses give you the law, and yet none of you keepeth the law? Why go ye about to kill me?

7:20 The people answered and said, Thou hast a devil: who goeth about to kill thee? 7:21 Jesus answered and said unto them, I have done one work, and ye all marvel. 7:22 Moses therefore gave unto you circumcision; (not because it is of Moses, but of the fathers;) and ye on the sabbath day circumcise a man. 7:23 If a man on the sabbath day receive circumcision, that the law of Moses should not be broken; are ye angry at me, because I have made a man every whit whole on the sabbath day? 7:24 Judge not according to the appearance, but judge righteous judgment. 7:25 Then said some of them of Jerusalem, Is not this he, whom they seek to kill? 7:26 But, lo, he speaketh boldly, and they say nothing unto him. Do the rulers know indeed that this is the very Christ? 7:27 Howbeit we know this man whence he is: but when Christ cometh, no man knoweth whence he is. 7:28 Then cried Jesus in the temple as he taught, saying, Ye both know me, and ye know whence

I am: and I am not come of myself, but he that sent me is true, whom ye know not. 7:29 But I know him: for I am from him, and he hath sent me. 7:30 Then they sought to take him: but no man laid hands on him, because his hour was not yet come. 7:31 And many of the people believed on him, and said, When Christ cometh, will he do more miracles than these which this man hath done?

7:32 The Pharisees heard that the people murmured such things concerning him; and the Pharisees and the chief priests sent officers to take him. 7:33 Then said Jesus unto them, Yet a little while am I with you, and then I go unto him that sent me.

7:34 Ye shall seek me, and shall not find me: and where I am, thither ye cannot come. 7:35 Then said the Jews among themselves, Whither will he go, that we shall not find him? Will he go unto the dispersed among the Gentiles, and teach the Gentiles? 7:36 What manner of saying is this that he said, Ye shall seek me, and shall not find me: and where I am, thither ye cannot come? 7:37 In the last day, that great day of the feast, Jesus stood and cried, saying, If any man thirst, let him come unto me, and drink. 7:38 He that believeth on me, as the scripture hath said, out of his belly shall flow rivers of living water. 7:39 (But this spake he of the Spirit, which they that believe on him should receive: for the Holy Ghost was not yet given; because that Jesus was not yet glorified.)

7:40 Many of the people therefore, when they heard this saying, said, Of a truth this is the Prophet. 7:41 Others said, This is the Christ. But some said, Shall Christ come out of Galilee? 7:42 Hath not the scripture said, That Christ cometh of the seed of David, and out of the town of Bethlehem, where David was? 7:43 So there was a division among the people because of him. 7:44 And some of them would have taken him; but no man laid hands on him. 7:45 Then came the officers to the chief priests and Pharisees; and they said unto them, Why have ye not brought him? 7:46 The officers answered, Never man spake like this man. 7:47 Then answered them the Pharisees, Are ye also deceived? 7:48 Have any of the rulers or of the Pharisees believed on him?

7:49 But this people who knoweth not the law are cursed.

7:50 Nicodemus saith unto them, (he that came to Jesus by night, being one of them,) 7:51 Doth our law judge any man, before it hear him, and know what he doeth? 7:52 They answered and said unto him, Art thou also of Galilee? Search, and look: for out of Galilee ariseth no prophet. 7:53 And every man went unto his own house.

Do Jesus words penetrate you as deeply as music?

_____
_____
_____
_____
_____
_____
_____

Filial Piety In Mourning For Parents from *The Hsiâo King*

The Master said, 'When a filial son is mourning for a parent, he wails, but not with a prolonged sobbing; in the movements of ceremony he pays no attention to his appearance; his words are without elegance of phrase; he cannot bear to wear fine clothes; when he bears music, he feels no delight; when he eats a delicacy, he is not conscious of its flavour: such is the nature of grief and sorrow.

Book One, Chapter One from *The Discourses* by Epictetus

Of all the faculties, you will find not one which is capable of contemplating itself; and, consequently, not capable either of approving or disapproving. How far does the grammatic art possess the contemplating power? As far as forming a judgement about what is written and spoken. And how far music? As far as judging about melody. Does either of them then contemplate itself? By no means. But when you must write something to your friend, grammar will tell you what words you must write; but whether you should write or not, grammar will not tell you. And so it is with music as to musical sounds; but whether you should sing at the present time and play on the lute, or do neither, music will not tell you. What faculty then will tell you? That which contemplates both itself and all other things. And what is this faculty? The rational faculty.

∞

Chapter Eight, Light & Motion

The Light of the World created light, just as the Artificer gave motion to the insides of creatures. The miracle of these aspects of creation is astounding. Light has been viewed as a wave, a particle, and as duality of wave and particle. Even now, we are not positive what the exact nature of light is. Part of this might be the fact that "God is light, and in him is no darkness at all" (1 John 1:5). Even more intriguing is the fact that motion is recorded before the creation of light. "The Spirit of God moved upon the face of the waters. And God said, Let there be light: and there was light" (Genesis 1:2-3). To further highlight this, realize that since God is Spirit, and He breathed the breath of life into man, that the internal motions of man are in relation to the Spirit of God, for the Spirit of God is known to move. The highest connection between motion and light is when the Spirit descends upon someone and gives light into their heart to understand the truth of God.

"In winter I get up at night
And dress by yellow candle-light.
In summer, quite the other way,
I have to go to bed by day."

Source: Stevenson, Robert Louis: "A Child's Garden of Verses"
Artist: Jessie Willcox Smith

~

8:1 Jesus went unto the mount of Olives. 8:2 And early in the morning he came again into the temple, and all the people came unto him; and he sat down, and taught them. 8:3 And the scribes and Pharisees brought unto him a woman taken in adultery; and when they had set her in the midst, 8:4 They say unto him, Master, this woman was taken in adultery, in the very act.

8:5 Now Moses in the law commanded us, that such should be stoned: but what sayest thou? 8:6 This they said, tempting him, that they might have to accuse him. But Jesus stooped down, and with his finger wrote on the ground, as though he heard them not. 8:7 So when they continued asking him, he lifted up himself, and said unto them, He that is without sin among you, let him first cast a stone at her.

8:8 And again he stooped down, and wrote on the ground.

8:9 And they which heard it, being convicted by their own conscience, went out one by one, beginning at the eldest, even unto the last: and Jesus was left alone, and the woman standing in the midst.

8:10 When Jesus had lifted up himself, and saw none but the woman, he said unto her, Woman, where are those thine accusers? hath no man condemned thee?

8:11 She said, No man, Lord. And Jesus said unto her, Neither do I condemn thee: go, and sin no more. 8:12 Then spake Jesus again unto them, saying, I am the light of the world: he that followeth me shall not walk in darkness, but shall have the light of life.

8:13 The Pharisees therefore said unto him, Thou bearest record of thyself; thy record is not true. 8:14 Jesus answered and said unto them, Though I bear record of myself, yet my record is true: for I know whence I came, and whither I go; but ye cannot tell whence I come, and whither I go. 8:15 Ye judge after the flesh; I judge no man.

8:16 And yet if I judge, my judgment is true: for I am not alone, but I and the Father that sent me. 8:17 It is also written in your law, that the testimony of two men is true. 8:18 I am one that bear witness of myself, and the Father that sent me beareth witness of me. 8:19 Then said they unto him, Where is thy Father? Jesus answered, Ye neither know me, nor my Father: if ye had known me, ye should have known my Father also.

8:20 These words spake Jesus in the treasury, as he taught in the temple: and no man laid hands on him; for his hour was not yet come.

8:21 Then said Jesus again unto them, I go my way, and ye shall seek me, and shall die in your sins: whither I go, ye cannot come.

8:22 Then said the Jews, Will he kill himself? because he saith, Whither I go, ye cannot come. 8:23 And he said unto them, Ye are from beneath; I am from above: ye are of this world; I am not of this world.

8:24 I said therefore unto you, that ye shall die in your sins: for if ye believe not that I am he, ye shall die in your sins. 8:25 Then said they unto him, Who art thou? And Jesus saith unto them, Even the same that I said unto you from the beginning. 8:26 I have many things to say and to judge of you: but he that sent me is true; and I speak to the world those things which I have heard of him. 8:27 They understood not that he spake to them of the Father. 8:28 Then said Jesus unto them, When ye have lifted up the Son of man, then shall ye know that I am he, and that I do nothing of myself; but as my Father hath taught me, I speak these things. 8:29 And he that sent me is with me: the Father hath not left me alone; for I do always those things that please him.

8:30 As he spake these words, many believed on him.

8:31 Then said Jesus to those Jews which believed on him, If ye continue in my word, then are ye my disciples indeed;

8:32 And ye shall know the truth, and the truth shall make you free.

8:33 They answered him, We be Abraham's seed, and were never in bondage to any man: how sayest thou, Ye shall be made free?

8:34 Jesus answered them, Verily, verily, I say unto you, Whosoever committeth sin is the servant of sin. 8:35 And the servant abideth not in the house for ever: but the Son abideth ever. 8:36 If the Son therefore shall make you free, ye shall be free indeed. 8:37 I know that ye are Abraham's seed; but ye seek to kill me, because my word hath no place in you. 8:38 I speak that which I have seen with my Father: and ye do that which ye have seen with your father. 8:39 They answered and said unto him, Abraham is our father. Jesus saith unto them, If ye were Abraham's children, ye would do the works of Abraham.

8:40 But now ye seek to kill me, a man that hath told you the truth, which I have heard of God: this did not Abraham.

8:41 Ye do the deeds of your father. Then said they to him, We be not born of fornication; we have one Father, even God.

8:42 Jesus said unto them, If God were your Father, ye would love me: for I proceeded forth and came from God; neither came I of myself, but he sent me. 8:43 Why do ye not understand my speech? even because ye cannot hear my word. 8:44 Ye are of your father the devil, and the lusts of your father ye will do. He was a murderer from the beginning, and abode not in the truth, because there is no truth in him. When he speaketh a lie, he speaketh of his own: for he is a liar, and the father of it. 8:45 And because I tell you the truth, ye believe me not.

8:46 Which of you convinceth me of sin? And if I say the truth, why do ye not believe me? 8:47 He that is of God heareth God's words: ye therefore hear them not, because ye are not of God.

8:48 Then answered the Jews, and said unto him, Say we not well that thou art a Samaritan, and hast a devil? 8:49 Jesus answered, I have not a devil; but I honour my Father, and ye do dishonour me. 8:50 And I seek not mine own glory: there is one that seeketh and judgeth.

8:51 Verily, verily, I say unto you, If a man keep my saying, he shall never see death. 8:52 Then said the Jews unto him, Now we know that thou hast a devil. Abraham is dead, and the prophets; and thou sayest, If a man keep my saying, he shall never taste of death.

8:53 Art thou greater than our father Abraham, which is dead? and the prophets are dead: whom makest thou thyself? 8:54 Jesus answered, If I honour myself, my honour is nothing: it is my Father that honoureth me; of whom ye say, that he is your God: 8:55 Yet ye have not known him; but I know him: and if I should say, I know him not, I shall be a liar like unto you: but I know him, and keep his saying.

8:56 Your father Abraham rejoiced to see my day: and he saw it, and was glad. 8:57 Then said the Jews unto him, Thou art not yet fifty years old, and hast thou seen Abraham? 8:58 Jesus said unto them, Verily, verily, I say unto you, Before Abraham was, I am. 8:59 Then took they up stones to cast at him: but Jesus hid himself, and went out of the temple, going through the midst of them, and so passed by.

Why did they want to stone Jesus?

_____
_____
_____
_____
_____
_____
_____

Introduction from *Leviathan*
by Thomas Hobbes

Nature (the art whereby God hath made and governs the world) is by the art of man, as in many other things, so in this also imitated, that it can make an artificial animal. For seeing life is but a motion of limbs, the beginning whereof is in some principal part within, why may we not say that all automata (engines that move themselves by springs and wheels as doth a watch) have an artificial life? For what is the heart, but a spring; and the nerves, but so many strings; and the joints, but so many wheels, giving motion to the whole body, such as was intended by the Artificer?

Antique Engraving of a Horse
Source: Joannes Jonstonus: "A description of the nature of four-footed beasts"

Chapter Nine, Blind

Blindness can make life hard to live, but being sightless can give one a true look at oneself and a great vision of God. When one has less distractions to get in their way, the clarity of one's sinfulness, and the glory of God has an easier time shining through. Jesus said, "If ye were blind, ye should have no sin: but now ye say, We see; therefore your sin remaineth"(John 9:41). Admitting that we have sin is the key to beginning a relationship with God, for now we can enter the door to God, Jesus Christ. Once in Jesus Christ, our sin is wiped away by his perfect sacrifice. He died in our place to bring us back to God. As the song Amazing Grace says best, "I once was lost but now am found, Was blind, but now, I see."

Swinging Corpse Silhouette
Source: Bill Nye "Bill Nye's History of England"
Cartoonist: W. M. Goodes

~

9:1 And as Jesus passed by, he saw a man which was blind from his birth. 9:2 And his disciples asked him, saying, Master, who did sin, this man, or his parents, that he was born blind?

135

9:3 Jesus answered, Neither hath this man sinned, nor his parents: but that the works of God should be made manifest in him.

9:4 I must work the works of him that sent me, while it is day: the night cometh, when no man can work. 9:5 As long as I am in the world, I am the light of the world. 9:6 When he had thus spoken, he spat on the ground, and made clay of the spittle, and he anointed the eyes of the blind man with the clay, 9:7 And said unto him, Go, wash in the pool of Siloam, (which is by interpretation, Sent.) He went his way therefore, and washed, and came seeing. 9:8 The neighbours therefore, and they which before had seen him that he was blind, said, Is not this he that sat and begged? 9:9 Some said, This is he: others said, He is like him: but he said, I am he. 9:10 Therefore said they unto him, How were thine eyes opened? 9:11 He answered and said, A man that is called Jesus made clay, and anointed mine eyes, and said unto me, Go to the pool of Siloam, and wash: and I went and washed, and I received sight.

9:12 Then said they unto him, Where is he? He said, I know not.

9:13 They brought to the Pharisees him that aforetime was blind.

9:14 And it was the sabbath day when Jesus made the clay, and opened his eyes. 9:15 Then again the Pharisees also asked him how he had received his sight. He said unto them, He put clay upon mine eyes, and I washed, and do see. 9:16 Therefore said some of the Pharisees, This man is not of God, because he keepeth not the sabbath day. Others said, How can a man that is a sinner do such miracles? And there was a division among them. 9:17 They say unto the blind man again, What sayest thou of him, that he hath opened thine eyes? He said, He is a prophet. 9:18 But the Jews did not believe concerning him, that he had been blind, and received his sight, until they called the parents of him that had received his sight. 9:19 And they asked them, saying, Is this your son, who ye say was born blind? how then doth he now see?

9:20 His parents answered them and said, We know that this is our son, and that he was born blind: 9:21 But by what means he now seeth, we know not; or who hath opened his eyes, we know not: he is of age; ask him: he shall speak for himself. 9:22 These words spake his parents, because they feared the Jews: for the Jews had agreed already, that if any man did confess that he was Christ, he should be put out of the synagogue. 9:23 Therefore said his parents, He is of age; ask him.

9:24 Then again called they the man that was blind, and said unto him, Give God the praise: we know that this man is a sinner.

9:25 He answered and said, Whether he be a sinner or no, I know not:

one thing I know, that, whereas I was blind, now I see.

9:26 Then said they to him again, What did he to thee? How opened he thine eyes? 9:27 He answered them, I have told you already, and ye did not hear: wherefore would ye hear it again? will ye also be his disciples? 9:28 Then they reviled him, and said, Thou art his disciple; but we are Moses' disciples.

9:29 We know that God spake unto Moses: as for this fellow, we know not from whence he is. 9:30 The man answered and said unto them, Why herein is a marvellous thing, that ye know not from whence he is, and yet he hath opened mine eyes.

9:31 Now we know that God heareth not sinners: but if any man be a worshipper of God, and doeth his will, him he heareth.

9:32 Since the world began was it not heard that any man opened the eyes of one that was born blind. 9:33 If this man were not of God, he could do nothing. 9:34 They answered and said unto him, Thou wast altogether born in sins, and dost thou teach us? And they cast him out.

9:35 Jesus heard that they had cast him out; and when he had found him, he said unto him, Dost thou believe on the Son of God?

9:36 He answered and said, Who is he, Lord, that I might believe on him? 9:37 And Jesus said unto him, Thou hast both seen him, and it is he that talketh with thee.

9:38 And he said, Lord, I believe. And he worshipped him.

9:39 And Jesus said, For judgment I am come into this world, that they which see not might see; and that they which see might be made blind. 9:40 And some of the Pharisees which were with him heard these words, and said unto him, Are we blind also?

9:41 Jesus said unto them, If ye were blind, ye should have no sin: but now ye say, We see; therefore your sin remaineth.

Why did Jesus use clay to make the blind man see?

_____
_____
_____
_____
_____
_____
_____

The Monadology
by Gottfried Wilhelm Leibniz

1. The Monad, of which we shall here speak, is nothing but a simple substance, which enters into compounds. By 'simple' is meant 'without parts.' (Theod. 10.)

86. This City of God, this truly universal monarchy, is a moral world in the natural world, and is the most exalted and most divine among the works of God; and it is in it that the glory of God really consists, for He would have no glory were not His greatness and His goodness known and admired by spirits [esprits]. It is also in relation to this divine City that God specially has goodness, while His wisdom and His power are manifested everywhere. (Theod. 146; Abrege, Object. 2.)

December

An old tonsured man wearing a monk's robe and a gown is supping lustily from a giant bowl of liquid. He rides a goat, representing the lasciviousness of the festivals at December.

Source: William Hone: "Hone's Everyday Book"

Chapter Ten, Sheep & A Door

Different doors lead to different places. This might seem like common-sense, but how feel realize that they are picking and choosing which doors to walk through every day, and that the consequences of these actions leads to an eternal home. Some doors lead to recesses of the imagination, other doors let monsters enter into castles, but only one door leads to eternal life, and His name is Jesus Christ. The daily doors are actions of either good or bad: Do you walk into a den of dirty dancing or do you step through the portal of helping others? Pick your daily doors wisely; make sure you have already entered the gate of the Shepherd.

"She tried the little golden key in the lock, and to her great delight it fitted!"

Source: Lewis Caroll "Alice's Adventures in Wonderland"
Artist: Sir John Tenniel

~

10:1 Verily, verily, I say unto you, He that entereth not by the door into the sheepfold, but climbeth up some other way, the same is a thief and a robber. 10:2 But he that entereth in by the door is the shepherd of the sheep. 10:3 To him the porter openeth; and the sheep hear his voice: and he calleth his own sheep by name, and leadeth them out.
10:4 And when he putteth forth his own sheep, he goeth before them,

and the sheep follow him: for they know his voice. 10:5 And a stranger will they not follow, but will flee from him: for they know not the voice of strangers. 10:6 This parable spake Jesus unto them: but they understood not what things they were which he spake unto them.

10:7 Then said Jesus unto them again, Verily, verily, I say unto you, I am the door of the sheep. 10:8 All that ever came before me are thieves and robbers: but the sheep did not hear them. 10:9 I am the door: by me if any man enter in, he shall be saved, and shall go in and out, and find pasture.

10:10 The thief cometh not, but for to steal, and to kill, and to destroy: I am come that they might have life, and that they might have it more abundantly. 10:11 I am the good shepherd: the good shepherd giveth his life for the sheep. 10:12 But he that is an hireling, and not the shepherd, whose own the sheep are not, seeth the wolf coming, and leaveth the sheep, and fleeth: and the wolf catcheth them, and scattereth the sheep.

10:13 The hireling fleeth, because he is an hireling, and careth not for the sheep. 10:14 I am the good shepherd, and know my sheep, and am known of mine. 10:15 As the Father knoweth me, even so know I the Father: and I lay down my life for the sheep.

10:16 And other sheep I have, which are not of this fold: them also I must bring, and they shall hear my voice; and there shall be one fold, and one shepherd. 10:17 Therefore doth my Father love me, because I lay down my life, that I might take it again.

10:18 No man taketh it from me, but I lay it down of myself. I have power to lay it down, and I have power to take it again. This commandment have I received of my Father. 10:19 There was a division therefore again among the Jews for these sayings.

10:20 And many of them said, He hath a devil, and is mad; why hear ye him? 10:21 Others said, These are not the words of him that hath a devil. Can a devil open the eyes of the blind? 10:22 And it was at Jerusalem the feast of the dedication, and it was winter.

10:23 And Jesus walked in the temple in Solomon's porch.

10:24 Then came the Jews round about him, and said unto him, How long dost thou make us to doubt? If thou be the Christ, tell us plainly. 10:25 Jesus answered them, I told you, and ye believed not: the works that I do in my Father's name, they bear witness of me.

10:26 But ye believe not, because ye are not of my sheep, as I said unto you. 10:27 My sheep hear my voice, and I know them, and they follow me: 10:28 And I give unto them eternal life; and they shall never perish, neither shall any man pluck them out of my hand.

10:29 My Father, which gave them me, is greater than all; and no man is able to pluck them out of my Father's hand. 10:30 I and my Father are one. 10:31 Then the Jews took up stones again to stone him.

10:32 Jesus answered them, Many good works have I shewed you from my Father; for which of those works do ye stone me?

10:33 The Jews answered him, saying, For a good work we stone thee not; but for blasphemy; and because that thou, being a man, makest thyself God. 10:34 Jesus answered them, Is it not written in your law, I said, Ye are gods? 10:35 If he called them gods, unto whom the word of God came, and the scripture cannot be broken; 10:36 Say ye of him, whom the Father hath sanctified, and sent into the world, Thou blasphemest; because I said, I am the Son of God? 10:37 If I do not the works of my Father, believe me not. 10:38 But if I do, though ye believe not me, believe the works: that ye may know, and believe, that the Father is in me, and I in him. 10:39 Therefore they sought again to take him: but he escaped out of their hand, 10:40 And went away again beyond Jordan into the place where John at first baptized; and there he abode. 10:41 And many resorted unto him, and said, John did no miracle: but all things that John spake of this man were true.

10:42 And many believed on him there.

What type of daily doors do you walk through?

_____
_____
_____
_____
_____
_____
_____

Chapter One of Beowulf from *Hero-Myths and Legends of the British Race*
by Maud Isabel Ebbutt

"This the dire mighty fiend, he who in darkness dwelt, Suffered with hatred fierce, that every day and night He heard the festal shouts loud in the lofty hall; Sound of harp echoed there, and gleeman's sweet song. Thus they lived joyously, fearing no angry foe Until the hellish fiend wrought them great woe. Grendel that ghost was called, grisly and terrible, Who, hateful wanderer, dwelt in the moorlands, The fens and wild fastnesses; the wretch for a while abode In homes of the giant-race, since God had cast him out. When night on the earth fell, Grendel departed To visit the lofty hall, now that the warlike Danes After the gladsome feast nightly slept in it. A fair troop of warrior-thanes guarding it found he; Heedlessly sleeping, they reeked not of sorrow. The demon of evil, the grim wight unholy, With his fierce ravening, greedily grasped them, Seized in their slumbering thirty right manly thanes; Thence he withdrew again, proud of his lifeless prey, Home to his hiding-place, bearing his booty, In peace to devour it."

Space for Your Own Poem:

Chapter Eleven, Pride & Humility

The Wizard of Oz was full of show, but empty in power; Jesus is humble and possess all might. Compared to the puffed up Wizard, Jesus "humbled himself, and became obedient unto death, even the death of the cross"(Philippians 2:8). The Wizard was not able to bring Dorthy home properly; Jesus raised Lazarus from the dead to bring him back home. Is the pleasure of eating like a pig (see General Remarks below) comparable to the magnificence of being in the presence of God? Is anxiety about sharing the Gospel more painful than the agony of the Damned (see Chapter One below)? Be mindful of comparisons between pride and humility, insatiability and satisfaction, and love and hate.

The Wizard of Oz
Source: Ruth Plumly Thompson: "The Gnome King of Oz"
Artist: John R. Neill

~

11:1 Now a certain man was sick, named Lazarus, of Bethany, the town of Mary and her sister Martha. 11:2 (It was that Mary which anointed the Lord with ointment, and wiped his feet with her hair, whose brother Lazarus was sick.) 11:3 Therefore his sisters sent unto him, saying, Lord, behold, he whom thou lovest is sick.

11:4 When Jesus heard that, he said, This sickness is not unto death, but for the glory of God, that the Son of God might be glorified thereby. 11:5 Now Jesus loved Martha, and her sister, and Lazarus.

11:6 When he had heard therefore that he was sick, he abode two days still in the same place where he was. 11:7 Then after that saith he to his disciples, Let us go into Judaea again. 11:8 His disciples say unto him, Master, the Jews of late sought to stone thee; and goest thou thither again?

11:9 Jesus answered, Are there not twelve hours in the day? If any man walk in the day, he stumbleth not, because he seeth the light of this world. 11:10 But if a man walk in the night, he stumbleth, because there is no light in him. 11:11 These things said he: and after that he saith unto them, Our friend Lazarus sleepeth; but I go, that I may awake him out of sleep. 11:12 Then said his disciples, Lord, if he sleep, he shall do well. 11:13 Howbeit Jesus spake of his death: but they thought that he had spoken of taking of rest in sleep. 11:14 Then said Jesus unto them plainly, Lazarus is dead. 11:15 And I am glad for your sakes that I was not there, to the intent ye may believe; nevertheless let us go unto him. 11:16 Then said Thomas, which is called Didymus, unto his fellow disciples, Let us also go, that we may die with him.

11:17 Then when Jesus came, he found that he had lain in the grave four days already. 11:18 Now Bethany was nigh unto Jerusalem, about fifteen furlongs off: 11:19 And many of the Jews came to Martha and Mary, to comfort them concerning their brother. 11:20 Then Martha, as soon as she heard that Jesus was coming, went and met him: but Mary sat still in the house. 11:21 Then said Martha unto Jesus, Lord, if thou hadst been here, my brother had not died. 11:22 But I know, that even now, whatsoever thou wilt ask of God, God will give it thee.

11:23 Jesus saith unto her, Thy brother shall rise again.

11:24 Martha saith unto him, I know that he shall rise again in the resurrection at the last day. 11:25 Jesus said unto her, I am the resurrection, and the life: he that believeth in me, though he were dead, yet shall he live: 11:26 And whosoever liveth and believeth in me shall never die. Believest thou this? 11:27 She saith unto him, Yea, Lord: I believe that thou art the Christ, the Son of God, which should come into the world. 11:28 And when she had so said, she went her way, and called Mary her sister secretly, saying, The Master is come, and calleth for thee. 11:29 As soon as she heard that, she arose quickly, and came unto him.

11:30 Now Jesus was not yet come into the town, but was in that place where Martha met him. 11:31 The Jews then which were with her in the house, and comforted her, when they saw Mary, that she rose up hastily and went out, followed her, saying, She goeth unto the grave to weep there. 11:32 Then when Mary was come where Jesus was, and saw him, she fell down at his feet, saying unto him, Lord, if thou hadst been here, my brother had not died. 11:33 When Jesus therefore saw her weeping, and the Jews also weeping which came with her, he groaned in the spirit, and was troubled, 11:34 And said, Where have ye laid him? They said unto him, Lord, come and see. 11:35 Jesus wept.

11:36 Then said the Jews, Behold how he loved him!

11:37 And some of them said, Could not this man, which opened the eyes of the blind, have caused that even this man should not have died?

11:38 Jesus therefore again groaning in himself cometh to the grave. It was a cave, and a stone lay upon it. 11:39 Jesus said, Take ye away the stone. Martha, the sister of him that was dead, saith unto him, Lord, by this time he stinketh: for he hath been dead four days.

11:40 Jesus saith unto her, Said I not unto thee, that, if thou wouldest believe, thou shouldest see the glory of God? 11:41 Then they took away the stone from the place where the dead was laid. And Jesus lifted up his eyes, and said, Father, I thank thee that thou hast heard me.

11:42 And I knew that thou hearest me always: but because of the people which stand by I said it, that they may believe that thou hast sent me. 11:43 And when he thus had spoken, he cried with a loud voice, Lazarus, come forth.

11:44 And he that was dead came forth, bound hand and foot with graveclothes: and his face was bound about with a napkin. Jesus saith unto them, Loose him, and let him go. 11:45 Then many of the Jews which came to Mary, and had seen the things which Jesus did, believed on him. 11:46 But some of them went their ways to the Pharisees, and told them what things Jesus had done. 11:47 Then gathered the chief priests and the Pharisees a council, and said, What do we? for this man doeth many miracles. 11:48 If we let him thus alone, all men will believe on him: and the Romans shall come and take away both our place and nation. 11:49 And one of them, named Caiaphas, being the high priest that same year, said unto them, Ye know nothing at all,

11:50 Nor consider that it is expedient for us, that one man should die for the people, and that the whole nation perish not.

11:51 And this spake he not of himself: but being high priest that year, he prophesied that Jesus should die for that nation;

11:52 And not for that nation only, but that also he should gather together in one the children of God that were scattered abroad.

11:53 Then from that day forth they took counsel together for to put him to death. 11:54 Jesus therefore walked no more openly among the Jews; but went thence unto a country near to the wilderness, into a city called Ephraim, and there continued with his disciples.

11:55 And the Jews' passover was nigh at hand: and many went out of the country up to Jerusalem before the passover, to purify themselves. 11:56 Then sought they for Jesus, and spake among themselves, as they stood in the temple, What think ye, that he will not come to the feast? 11:57 Now both the chief priests and the Pharisees had given a commandment, that, if any man knew where he were, he should shew it, that they might take him.

How are you proud? How are you humble?

_____
_____
_____
_____
_____
_____
_____

Chapter One from *The Book of the Damned* By Charles Fort

Some of them are corpses, skeletons, mummies, twitching, tottering, animated by companions that have been damned alive. There are giants that will walk by, though sound asleep. There are things that are theorems and things that are rags: they'll go by like Euclid arm in arm with the spirit of anarchy. Here and there will flit little harlots. Many are clowns. But many are of the highest respectability. Some are assassins. There are pale stenches and gaunt superstitions and mere shadows and lively malices: whims and amiabilities. The naïve and the pedantic and the bizarre and the grotesque and the sincere and the insincere, the profound and the puerile.

General Remarks from Chapter One from *Utilitarianism* by John Stuart Mill

It is better to be a human being dissatisfied than a pig satisfied; better to be Socrates dissatisfied than a fool satisfied. And if the fool, or the pig, are a different opinion, it is because they only know their own side of the question. The other party to the comparison knows both sides.

ST. SIMEON STYLITES, HERMIT OF THE PILLAR.

Saint Simon, partly bald but with a long flowing beard, kneels barefoot on the top of a pillar and holds up a cross. He is wearing sackcloth.

Source: William Hone: "Hone's Everyday Book"

Chapter Twelve, Traditions

Whether it be the traditions of men in Masonry or the regulations of the Pharisees, or the customs of fanciful peoples as told in Alice in Wonderland, these rituals can get in the way of a relationship with God. In order to keep men happy, one must keep their traditions. Pleasing man was a thorn in the flesh for some of the Pharisees. They could have openly acknowledged Jesus, but instead they risked what Jesus warned about. Jesus said, "Whosoever shall deny me before men, him will I also deny before my Father which is in heaven"(Matthew 10:33). These Pharisees were willing to deny Jesus before men "For they loved the praise of men more than the praise of God"(John 12:43).

"The Mad Hatter runs out of court in his socks, carrying a sandwich and a bitten teacup."

Source: Lewis Caroll: "Alice's Adventures in Wonderland"
Artist: Sir John Tenniel

~

12:1 Then Jesus six days before the passover came to Bethany, where Lazarus was which had been dead, whom he raised from the dead.

12:2 There they made him a supper; and Martha served: but Lazarus was one of them that sat at the table with him.

12:3 Then took Mary a pound of ointment of spikenard, very costly, and anointed the feet of Jesus, and wiped his feet with her hair: and the house was filled with the odour of the ointment.

12:4 Then saith one of his disciples, Judas Iscariot, Simon's son, which should betray him, 12:5 Why was not this ointment sold for three hundred pence, and given to the poor? 12:6 This he said, not that he cared for the poor; but because he was a thief, and had the bag, and bare what was put therein. 12:7 Then said Jesus, Let her alone: against the day of my burying hath she kept this.

12:8 For the poor always ye have with you; but me ye have not always. 12:9 Much people of the Jews therefore knew that he was there: and they came not for Jesus' sake only, but that they might see Lazarus also, whom he had raised from the dead.

12:10 But the chief priests consulted that they might put Lazarus also to death; 12:11 Because that by reason of him many of the Jews went away, and believed on Jesus. 12:12 On the next day much people that were come to the feast, when they heard that Jesus was coming to Jerusalem, 12:13 Took branches of palm trees, and went forth to meet him, and cried, Hosanna: Blessed is the King of Israel that cometh in the name of the Lord.

12:14 And Jesus, when he had found a young ass, sat thereon; as it is written, 12:15 Fear not, daughter of Sion: behold, thy King cometh, sitting on an ass's colt. 12:16 These things understood not his disciples at the first: but when Jesus was glorified, then remembered they that these things were written of him, and that they had done these things unto him. 12:17 The people therefore that was with him when he called Lazarus out of his grave, and raised him from the dead, bare record. 12:18 For this cause the people also met him, for that they heard that he had done this miracle. 12:19 The Pharisees therefore said among themselves, Perceive ye how ye prevail nothing? behold, the world is gone after him. 12:20 And there were certain Greeks among them that came up to worship at the feast: 12:21 The same came therefore to Philip, which was of Bethsaida of Galilee, and desired him, saying, Sir, we would see Jesus. 12:22 Philip cometh and telleth Andrew: and again Andrew and Philip tell Jesus.

12:23 And Jesus answered them, saying, The hour is come, that the Son of man should be glorified. 12:24 Verily, verily, I say unto you, Except a corn of wheat fall into the ground and die, it abideth alone: but if it die, it bringeth forth much fruit.

12:25 He that loveth his life shall lose it; and he that hateth his life in this world shall keep it unto life eternal. 12:26 If any man serve me, let him follow me; and where I am, there shall also my servant be: if any man serve me, him will my Father honour. 12:27 Now is my soul troubled; and what shall I say? Father, save me from this hour: but for this cause came I unto this hour. 12:28 Father, glorify thy name. Then came there a voice from heaven, saying, I have both glorified it, and will glorify it again. 12:29 The people therefore, that stood by, and heard it, said that it thundered: others said, An angel spake to him.

12:30 Jesus answered and said, This voice came not because of me, but for your sakes. 12:31 Now is the judgment of this world: now shall the prince of this world be cast out. 12:32 And I, if I be lifted up from the earth, will draw all men unto me.

12:33 This he said, signifying what death he should die.

12:34 The people answered him, We have heard out of the law that Christ abideth for ever: and how sayest thou, The Son of man must be lifted up? who is this Son of man? 12:35 Then Jesus said unto them, Yet a little while is the light with you. Walk while ye have the light, lest darkness come upon you: for he that walketh in darkness knoweth not whither he goeth. 12:36 While ye have light, believe in the light, that ye may be the children of light. These things spake Jesus, and departed, and did hide himself from them. 12:37 But though he had done so many miracles before them, yet they believed not on him:

12:38 That the saying of Esaias the prophet might be fulfilled, which he spake, Lord, who hath believed our report? and to whom hath the arm of the Lord been revealed? 12:39 Therefore they could not believe, because that Esaias said again, 12:40 He hath blinded their eyes, and hardened their heart; that they should not see with their eyes, nor understand with their heart, and be converted, and I should heal them. 12:41 These things said Esaias, when he saw his glory, and spake of him. 12:42 Nevertheless among the chief rulers also many believed on him; but because of the Pharisees they did not confess him, lest they should be put out of the synagogue:

12:43 For they loved the praise of men more than the praise of God. 12:44 Jesus cried and said, He that believeth on me, believeth not on me, but on him that sent me. 12:45 And he that seeth me seeth him that sent me. 12:46 I am come a light into the world, that whosoever believeth on me should not abide in darkness. 12:47 And if any man hear my words, and believe not, I judge him not: for I came not to judge the world, but to save the world. 12:48 He that rejecteth me, and receiveth not my words, hath one that judgeth him: the word that I have spoken, the same shall judge him in the last day. 12:49 For I have not spoken of myself; but the Father which sent me, he gave me a commandment, what I should say, and what I should speak.

12:50 And I know that his commandment is life everlasting: whatsoever I speak therefore, even as the Father said unto me, so I speak.

What vain traditions do you keep because you love the praise of man more than the praise of God?

_____

_____

_____

_____

_____

_____

_____

Free-Masons from Chapter One from *The Builders*
By Joseph Fort Newton

From the foregoing pages it must be evident that Masonry, as we find it in the Middle Ages, was not a novelty. Already, if we accept its own records, it was hoary with age, having come down from a far past, bringing with it a remarkable deposit of legendary lore. Also, it had in its keeping the same simple, eloquent emblems which, as we have seen, are older than the oldest living religion, which it received as an inheritance and has transmitted as a treasure. Whatever we may think of the legends of Masonry, as recited in its oldest documents, its symbols, older than the order itself, link it with the earliest thought and faith of the race. No doubt those emblems lost some of their luster in the troublous time of transition we are about to traverse, but their beauty never wholly faded, and they had only to be touched to shine.

Prologue from Thus Spake Zarathustra
by Friedrich Nietzsche

1. When Zarathustra was thirty years old, he left his home and the lake of his home, and went into the mountains. There he enjoyed his spirit and his solitude, and for ten years did not weary of it. But at last

his heart changed,- and rising one morning with the rosy dawn, he went before the sun, and spake thus unto it: Thou great star! What would be thy happiness if thou hadst not those for whom thou shinest! For ten years hast thou climbed hither unto my cave: thou wouldst have wearied of thy light and of the journey, had it not been for me, mine eagle, and my serpent. But we awaited thee every morning, took from thee thine overflow, and blessed thee for it.

8. When Zarathustra had said this to his heart, he put the corpse upon his shoulders and set out on his way. Yet had he not gone a hundred steps, when there stole a man up to him and whispered in his ear- and lo! he that spake was the buffoon from the tower. "Leave this town, O Zarathustra," said he, "there are too many here who hate thee. The good and just hate thee, and call thee their enemy and despiser; the believers in the orthodox belief hate thee, and call thee a danger to the multitude. It was thy good fortune to be laughed at: and verily thou spakest like a buffoon. It was thy good fortune to associate with the dead dog; by so humiliating thyself thou hast saved thy life to-day. Depart, however, from this town,- or tomorrow I shall jump over thee, a living man over a dead one." And when he had said this, the buffoon vanished; Zarathustra, however, went on through the dark streets.

White Rabbit, dressed as herald, blowing trumpet
Source: Lewis Caroll: "Alice's Adventures in Wonderland"
Artist: Sir John Tenniel
Engraver: Dalziel

Chapter Thirteen, Food

Food is central to fellowship. Many fond memories are formed around the dinner table, no matter your mind be one of logic or of intuition. A telling sign of the strength of the Christian is whether they thank God for their food before they eat, even with unbelievers at the table. One does not often desire to cause harm to someone sitting at the table with you, but in the case of Judas Iscariot, he did not have concern over what his actions would do to Jesus. Use meal time as a time of friendship and not as a time of plotting against your companions.

Biddy

"It is very nice to think
The world is full of meat and drink,
With little children saying grace
In every Christian kind of place."

Source: Robert Louis Stevenson: "A Child's Garden of Verses"
Artist: Jessie Willcox Smith (1863-1935)

~

13:1 Now before the feast of the passover, when Jesus knew that his hour was come that he should depart out of this world unto the Father, having loved his own which were in the world, he loved them unto the end. 13:2 And supper being ended, the devil having now put into the heart of Judas Iscariot, Simon's son, to betray him;
13:3 Jesus knowing that the Father had given all things into his hands, and that he was come from God, and went to God;

153

13:4 He riseth from supper, and laid aside his garments; and took a towel, and girded himself. 13:5 After that he poureth water into a bason, and began to wash the disciples' feet, and to wipe them with the towel wherewith he was girded. 13:6 Then cometh he to Simon Peter: and Peter saith unto him, Lord, dost thou wash my feet?

13:7 Jesus answered and said unto him, What I do thou knowest not now; but thou shalt know hereafter.

13:8 Peter saith unto him, Thou shalt never wash my feet. Jesus answered him, If I wash thee not, thou hast no part with me.

13:9 Simon Peter saith unto him, Lord, not my feet only, but also my hands and my head. 13:10 Jesus saith to him, He that is washed needeth not save to wash his feet, but is clean every whit: and ye are clean, but not all. 13:11 For he knew who should betray him; therefore said he, Ye are not all clean.

13:12 So after he had washed their feet, and had taken his garments, and was set down again, he said unto them, Know ye what I have done to you? 13:13 Ye call me Master and Lord: and ye say well; for so I am. 13:14 If I then, your Lord and Master, have washed your feet; ye also ought to wash one another's feet. 13:15 For I have given you an example, that ye should do as I have done to you. 13:16 Verily, verily, I say unto you, The servant is not greater than his lord; neither he that is sent greater than he that sent him. 13:17 If ye know these things, happy are ye if ye do them. 13:18 I speak not of you all: I know whom I have chosen: but that the scripture may be fulfilled, He that eateth bread with me hath lifted up his heel against me. 13:19 Now I tell you before it come, that, when it is come to pass, ye may believe that I am he.

13:20 Verily, verily, I say unto you, He that receiveth whomsoever I send receiveth me; and he that receiveth me receiveth him that sent me. 13:21 When Jesus had thus said, he was troubled in spirit, and testified, and said, Verily, verily, I say unto you, that one of you shall betray me. 13:22 Then the disciples looked one on another, doubting of whom he spake. 13:23 Now there was leaning on Jesus' bosom one of his disciples, whom Jesus loved. 13:24 Simon Peter therefore beckoned to him, that he should ask who it should be of whom he spake.

13:25 He then lying on Jesus' breast saith unto him, Lord, who is it? 13:26 Jesus answered, He it is, to whom I shall give a sop, when I have dipped it. And when he had dipped the sop, he gave it to Judas Iscariot, the son of Simon. 13:27 And after the sop Satan entered into him. Then said Jesus unto him, That thou doest, do quickly. 13:28 Now no man at the table knew for what intent he spake this unto him.

13:29 For some of them thought, because Judas had the bag, that Jesus had said unto him, Buy those things that we have need of against the feast; or, that he should give something to the poor.

13:30 He then having received the sop went immediately out: and it was night. 13:31 Therefore, when he was gone out, Jesus said, Now is the Son of man glorified, and God is glorified in him. 13:32 If God be glorified in him, God shall also glorify him in himself, and shall straightway glorify him. 13:33 Little children, yet a little while I am with you. Ye shall seek me: and as I said unto the Jews, Whither I go, ye cannot come; so now I say to you.

13:34 A new commandment I give unto you, That ye love one another; as I have loved you, that ye also love one another. 13:35 By this shall all men know that ye are my disciples, if ye have love one to another.

13:36 Simon Peter said unto him, Lord, whither goest thou? Jesus answered him, Whither I go, thou canst not follow me now; but thou shalt follow me afterwards. 13:37 Peter said unto him, Lord, why cannot I follow thee now? I will lay down my life for thy sake.

13:38 Jesus answered him, Wilt thou lay down thy life for my sake? Verily, verily, I say unto thee, The cock shall not crow, till thou hast denied me thrice.

Have you prepared food for friends? Why?

_____
_____
_____
_____
_____
_____
_____

Natural Causes Of Lycanthropy from *The Book Of Were-Wolves*
by Sabine Baring-Gould

It is positively true that there are many to whom the sight of suffering causes genuine pleasure, and in whom the passion to kill or torture is as strong as any other passion. Witness the number of boys who assemble around a sheep or pig when it is about to be killed, and who watch the struggle of the dying brute with hearts beating fast with pleasure, and eyes sparkling with delight. Often have I seen an eager crowd of children assembled around the slaughterhouses of French towns, absorbed in the expiring agonies of the sheep and cattle, and hushed into silence as they watched the flow of blood.

Thoughts on Mind and on Style from *Pensees* by Blaise Pascal

The difference between the mathematical and the intuitive mind. In the one, the principles are palpable, but removed from ordinary use; so that for want of habit it is difficult to turn one's mind in that direction: but if one turns it thither ever so little, one sees the principles fully, and one must have a quite inaccurate mind who reasons wrongly from principles so plain that it is almost impossible they should escape notice. But in the intuitive mind the principles are found in common use and are before the eyes of everybody. One has only to look, and no effort is necessary; it is only a question of good eyesight, but it must be good, for the principles are so subtle and so numerous that it is almost impossible but that some escape notice. Now the omission of one principle leads to error; thus one must have very clear sight to see all the principles and, in the next place, an accurate mind not to draw false deductions from known principles.

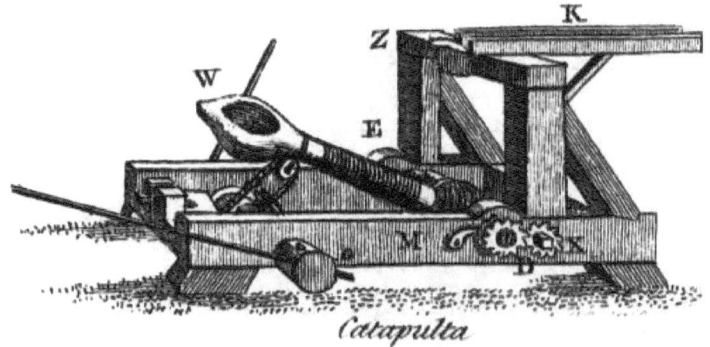

Catapulta

Source: Francis Grose: "The Antiquities of England and Wales"

Chapter Fourteen, Sin

The taking away of sin can only be done by a sinless sacrifice that is in the same form as the sinner, for the likeness of the sinner must be in the sacrifice for the punishment to be transferred from one to the other. Ocean gods or fruit sacrifices can never take away iniquity or the breaking of the law as exemplified in the Ten Commandments. One must be in the Son, who is in the Father; and the Son must be in you.

Chapter Head of Clerk Colvill
Source: Arthur Rackham "Some British Ballads"

~

14:1 Let not your heart be troubled: ye believe in God, believe also in me. 14:2 In my Father's house are many mansions: if it were not so, I would have told you. I go to prepare a place for you. 14:3 And if I go and prepare a place for you, I will come again, and receive you unto myself; that where I am, there ye may be also. 14:4 And whither I go ye know, and the way ye know. 14:5 Thomas saith unto him, Lord, we know not whither thou goest; and how can we know the way?
14:6 Jesus saith unto him, I am the way, the truth, and the life: no man cometh unto the Father, but by me. 14:7 If ye had known me, ye should have known my Father also: and from henceforth ye know him, and have seen him. 14:8 Philip saith unto him, Lord, shew us the Father, and

it sufficeth us. 14:9 Jesus saith unto him, Have I been so long time with you, and yet hast thou not known me, Philip? he that hath seen me hath seen the Father; and how sayest thou then, Shew us the Father?

14:10 Believest thou not that I am in the Father, and the Father in me? The words that I speak unto you I speak not of myself: but the Father that dwelleth in me, he doeth the works. 14:11 Believe me that I am in the Father, and the Father in me: or else believe me for the very works' sake. 14:12 Verily, verily, I say unto you, He that believeth on me, the works that I do shall he do also; and greater works than these shall he do; because I go unto my Father. 14:13 And whatsoever ye shall ask in my name, that will I do, that the Father may be glorified in the Son. 14:14 If ye shall ask any thing in my name, I will do it.

14:15 If ye love me, keep my commandments. 14:16 And I will pray the Father, and he shall give you another Comforter, that he may abide with you for ever; 14:17 Even the Spirit of truth; whom the world cannot receive, because it seeth him not, neither knoweth him: but ye know him; for he dwelleth with you, and shall be in you. 14:18 I will not leave you comfortless: I will come to you. 14:19 Yet a little while, and the world seeth me no more; but ye see me: because I live, ye shall live also. 14:20 At that day ye shall know that I am in my Father, and ye in me, and I in you. 14:21 He that hath my commandments, and keepeth them, he it is that loveth me: and he that loveth me shall be loved of my Father, and I will love him, and will manifest myself to him.

14:22 Judas saith unto him, not Iscariot, Lord, how is it that thou wilt manifest thyself unto us, and not unto the world?

14:23 Jesus answered and said unto him, If a man love me, he will keep my words: and my Father will love him, and we will come unto him, and make our abode with him. 14:24 He that loveth me not keepeth not my sayings: and the word which ye hear is not mine, but the Father's which sent me.

14:25 These things have I spoken unto you, being yet present with you. 14:26 But the Comforter, which is the Holy Ghost, whom the Father will send in my name, he shall teach you all things, and bring all things to your remembrance, whatsoever I have said unto you.

14:27 Peace I leave with you, my peace I give unto you: not as the world giveth, give I unto you. Let not your heart be troubled, neither let it be afraid. 14:28 Ye have heard how I said unto you, I go away, and come again unto you. If ye loved me, ye would rejoice, because I said, I go unto the Father: for my Father is greater than I. 14:29 And now I have told you before it come to pass, that, when it is come to pass, ye might believe. 14:30 Hereafter I will not talk much with you: for the prince of this world cometh, and hath nothing in me. 14:31 But that the world may know that I love the Father; and as the Father gave me commandment, even so I do. Arise, let us go hence.

What have you asked for in Jesus' name? Why?

_____
_____
_____
_____
_____
_____
_____

Placing of the Shri-patra, Homa, Formation of the Chakra, and other Rites from *Mahanirvana Tantra* Translated by Sir John Woodroffe

There are also three kinds of parched food, superior, middle, and inferior. The excellent and pleasing kind is that made from Shali rice, white as a moonbeam, or from barley or wheat, and which has been fried in clarified butter. The middling variety is made of fried paddy. Other kinds of fried grain are inferior. Meat, fish, and parched food, fruits and roots, or anything else offered to the Devata along with wine, are called Shuddhi. O Devi! the offering of wine without Shuddhi, as also puja and tarpana (without Shuddhi), become fruitless, and the Devata is not propitiated. The drinking of wine without Shuddhi is like the swallowing of poison. The disciple is ever ailing, and lives for a short time and dies. O Great Devi! when the weakness of the Kali Age becomes great, one's own Shakti or wife should alone be known as the fifth Tattva. This is devoid of all defects. O Beloved of My Life! in this (the last Tattva) I have spoken of Svayambhu and other kinds of flower. As substitutes for them, however, I enjoin red sandal paste. Neither the Tattvas nor flowers, leaves, and fruits should be offered to the Mahadevi unless purified. The man who offers them without purification goes to hell.

The Ten Commandments contained in Chapter Twenty from *Exodus* by Moses

1 And God spake all these words, saying,

2 I am the LORD thy God, which have brought thee out of the land of Egypt, out of the house of bondage.

3 Thou shalt have no other gods before me.

4 Thou shalt not make unto thee any graven image, or any likeness of any thing that is in heaven above, or that is in the earth beneath, or that is in the water under the earth.

5 Thou shalt not bow down thyself to them, nor serve them: for I the LORD thy God am a jealous God, visiting the iniquity of the fathers upon the children unto the third and fourth generation of them that hate me;

6 And shewing mercy unto thousands of them that love me, and keep my commandments.

7 Thou shalt not take the name of the LORD thy God in vain; for the LORD will not hold him guiltless that taketh his name in vain.

8 Remember the sabbath day, to keep it holy.

9 Six days shalt thou labour, and do all thy work:

10 But the seventh day is the sabbath of the LORD thy God: in it thou shalt not do any work, thou, nor thy son, nor thy daughter, thy manservant, nor thy maidservant, nor thy cattle, nor thy stranger that is within thy gates:

11 For in six days the LORD made heaven and earth, the sea, and all that in them is, and rested the seventh day: wherefore the LORD blessed the sabbath day, and hallowed it.

12 Honour thy father and thy mother: that thy days may be long upon the land which the LORD thy God giveth thee.

13 Thou shalt not kill.

14 Thou shalt not commit adultery.

15 Thou shalt not steal.

16 Thou shalt not bear false witness against thy neighbour.

17 Thou shalt not covet thy neighbour's house, thou shalt not covet thy neighbour's wife, nor his manservant, nor his maidservant, nor his ox, nor his ass, nor any thing that is thy neighbour's.

18 And all the people saw the thunderings, and the lightnings, and the noise of the trumpet, and the mountain smoking: and when the people saw it, they removed, and stood afar off.

Have you broken any of the Ten Commandments?

_____

_____

_____

_____

_____

_____

_____

Moses Views the Promised Land
Source: The Brothers Dalziel: "A Record of Fifty Years' Work"
Engraver: Dalziel
Drawer: Lord Leighton

Chapter Fifteen, Punishment

There is a vast difference between the punishment of the guilty and of the innocent. Whether it be the locking up of someone in a torque, or the beating of a boy, or the death sentence of Socrates, pain is involved in chastisement. Mormon doctrine appears clear on the surface, but upon digging deeper fiction is found. Research for yourself the traits of the truth and the clues of a cult.

Captive Wearing the Torque.
Source: Charles Knight: "Old England: A Pictorial Museum"

~

15:1 I am the true vine, and my Father is the husbandman.
15:2 Every branch in me that beareth not fruit he taketh away: and every branch that beareth fruit, he purgeth it, that it may bring forth more fruit. 15:3 Now ye are clean through the word which I have spoken unto you. 15:4 Abide in me, and I in you. As the branch cannot bear fruit of itself, except it abide in the vine; no more can ye, except ye abide in me. 15:5 I am the vine, ye are the branches: He that abideth in me, and I in him, the same bringeth forth much fruit: for without me ye can do nothing. 15:6 If a man abide not in me, he is cast forth as a

branch, and is withered; and men gather them, and cast them into the fire, and they are burned. 15:7 If ye abide in me, and my words abide in you, ye shall ask what ye will, and it shall be done unto you.

15:8 Herein is my Father glorified, that ye bear much fruit; so shall ye be my disciples. 15:9 As the Father hath loved me, so have I loved you: continue ye in my love. 15:10 If ye keep my commandments, ye shall abide in my love; even as I have kept my Father's commandments, and abide in his love.

15:11 These things have I spoken unto you, that my joy might remain in you, and that your joy might be full. 15:12 This is my commandment, That ye love one another, as I have loved you. 15:13 Greater love hath no man than this, that a man lay down his life for his friends.

15:14 Ye are my friends, if ye do whatsoever I command you.

15:15 Henceforth I call you not servants; for the servant knoweth not what his lord doeth: but I have called you friends; for all things that I have heard of my Father I have made known unto you.

15:16 Ye have not chosen me, but I have chosen you, and ordained you, that ye should go and bring forth fruit, and that your fruit should remain: that whatsoever ye shall ask of the Father in my name, he may give it you. 15:17 These things I command you, that ye love one another. 15:18 If the world hate you, ye know that it hated me before it hated you.

15:19 If ye were of the world, the world would love his own: but because ye are not of the world, but I have chosen you out of the world, therefore the world hateth you. 15:20 Remember the word that I said unto you, The servant is not greater than his lord. If they have persecuted me, they will also persecute you; if they have kept my saying, they will keep yours also. 15:21 But all these things will they do unto you for my name's sake, because they know not him that sent me. 15:22 If I had not come and spoken unto them, they had not had sin: but now they have no cloke for their sin. 15:23 He that hateth me hateth my Father also. 15:24 If I had not done among them the works which none other man did, they had not had sin: but now have they both seen and hated both me and my Father. 15:25 But this cometh to pass, that the word might be fulfilled that is written in their law, They hated me without a cause. 15:26 But when the Comforter is come, whom I will send unto you from the Father, even the Spirit of truth, which proceedeth from the Father, he shall testify of me: 15:27 And ye also shall bear witness, because ye have been with me from the beginning.

How does the world hate or punish you?

_____
_____
_____
_____
_____
_____
_____

Mormon Doctrine & Covenants
by Joseph F. Smith

1 On the third of October, in the year nineteen hundred and eighteen, I sat in my room pondering over the scriptures; 2 And reflecting upon the great atoning sacrifice that was made by the Son of God, for the redemption of the world; 3 And the great and wonderful love made manifest by the Father and the Son in the coming of the Redeemer into the world; 4 That through his atonement, and by obedience to the principles of the gospel, mankind might be saved.

Crito
by Plato

Scene: The Prison of Socrates.
Socrates. Why have you come at this hour, Crito? It must be quite early.
Crito. Yes, certainly.
Soc. What is the exact time?
Cr. The dawn is breaking.
Soc. I wonder the keeper of the prison would let you in.
Cr. He knows me because I often come, Socrates; moreover. I have done him a kindness.
Soc. And are you only just come?
Cr. No, I came some time ago.
Soc. Then why did you sit and say nothing, instead of awakening me at once?
Cr. Why, indeed, Socrates, I myself would rather not have all this

sleeplessness and sorrow. But I have been wondering at your peaceful slumbers, and that was the reason why I did not awaken you, because I wanted you to be out of pain. I have always thought you happy in the calmness of your temperament; but never did I see the like of the easy, cheerful way in which you bear this calamity.

Soc. Why, Crito, when a man has reached my age he ought not to be repining at the prospect of death.

Cr. And yet other old men find themselves in similar misfortunes, and age does not prevent them from repining.

Soc. That may be. But you have not told me why you have come at this early hour.

Beating the Boy
Source: Frédéric Goupil: "Les Aventures de Jean-Paul Choppart par Louis Desnoyers: L'Episode de Panouille"
Illustrator: Gérard-Séguin

165

Chapter Sixteen, Death

Unless Jesus comes back before you die, death is a certainty. There is no escaping the jaws of the grave. Just as Socrates died by poison and the suitors of Penelope at the hands of Odysseus, so all people will die of a cause. Man was originally meant to live forever without death, but by choosing to sin, we chose mortality. To bring about eternal life, a redeemer needed to die in our place. For the redeemed, death has lost its sting; For the saved, dieing is a doorway to eternity.

"A sketch of a curly-haired scruffily-dressed boy with his hands in his pockets."

Source: Frédéric Goupil: "Les Aventures de Jean-Paul Choppart par Louis Desnoyers: L'Episode de Panouille"
Illustrator: Gérard-Séguin
Engraver: Andrew Best

~

16:1 These things have I spoken unto you, that ye should not be offended. 16:2 They shall put you out of the synagogues: yea, the time cometh, that whosoever killeth you will think that he doeth God service. 16:3 And these things will they do unto you, because they have not known the Father, nor me. 16:4 But these things have I told you, that when the time shall come, ye may remember that I told you of them.

166

And these things I said not unto you at the beginning, because I was with you. 16:5 But now I go my way to him that sent me; and none of you asketh me, Whither goest thou? 16:6 But because I have said these things unto you, sorrow hath filled your heart. 16:7 Nevertheless I tell you the truth; It is expedient for you that I go away: for if I go not away, the Comforter will not come unto you; but if I depart, I will send him unto you. 16:8 And when he is come, he will reprove the world of sin, and of righteousness, and of judgment: 16:9 Of sin, because they believe not on me; 16:10 Of righteousness, because I go to my Father, and ye see me no more; 16:11 Of judgment, because the prince of this world is judged. 16:12 I have yet many things to say unto you, but ye cannot bear them now. 16:13 Howbeit when he, the Spirit of truth, is come, he will guide you into all truth: for he shall not speak of himself; but whatsoever he shall hear, that shall he speak: and he will shew you things to come.

16:14 He shall glorify me: for he shall receive of mine, and shall shew it unto you. 16:15 All things that the Father hath are mine: therefore said I, that he shall take of mine, and shall shew it unto you.

16:16 A little while, and ye shall not see me: and again, a little while, and ye shall see me, because I go to the Father.

16:17 Then said some of his disciples among themselves, What is this that he saith unto us, A little while, and ye shall not see me: and again, a little while, and ye shall see me: and, Because I go to the Father?

16:18 They said therefore, What is this that he saith, A little while? we cannot tell what he saith. 16:19 Now Jesus knew that they were desirous to ask him, and said unto them, Do ye enquire among yourselves of that I said, A little while, and ye shall not see me: and again, a little while, and ye shall see me? 16:20 Verily, verily, I say unto you, That ye shall weep and lament, but the world shall rejoice: and ye shall be sorrowful, but your sorrow shall be turned into joy.

16:21 A woman when she is in travail hath sorrow, because her hour is come: but as soon as she is delivered of the child, she remembereth no more the anguish, for joy that a man is born into the world.

16:22 And ye now therefore have sorrow: but I will see you again, and your heart shall rejoice, and your joy no man taketh from you.

16:23 And in that day ye shall ask me nothing. Verily, verily, I say unto you, Whatsoever ye shall ask the Father in my name, he will give it you.

16:24 Hitherto have ye asked nothing in my name: ask, and ye shall receive, that your joy may be full.

16:25 These things have I spoken unto you in proverbs: but the time cometh, when I shall no more speak unto you in proverbs, but I shall shew you plainly of the Father. 16:26 At that day ye shall ask in my name: and I say not unto you, that I will pray the Father for you:

16:27 For the Father himself loveth you, because ye have loved me, and have believed that I came out from God. 16:28 I came forth from the Father, and am come into the world: again, I leave the world, and go to the Father. 16:29 His disciples said unto him, Lo, now speakest thou plainly, and speakest no proverb. 16:30 Now are we sure that thou knowest all things, and needest not that any man should ask thee: by this we believe that thou camest forth from God. 16:31 Jesus answered them, Do ye now believe? 16:32 Behold, the hour cometh, yea, is now come, that ye shall be scattered, every man to his own, and shall leave me alone: and yet I am not alone, because the Father is with me.

16:33 These things I have spoken unto you, that in me ye might have peace. In the world ye shall have tribulation: but be of good cheer; I have overcome the world.

How has the Comforter worked in your life?

_____
_____
_____
_____
_____
_____
_____

Phaedo
by Plato

The End of Socrates

When we heard that, we were ashamed, and refrained our tears; and he walked about until, as he said, his legs began to fail, and then he lay on his back, according to the directions, and the man who gave him the poison now and then looked at his feet and legs; and after a while he

168

pressed his foot hard and asked him if he could feel; and he said, no; and then his leg, and so upwards and upwards, and showed us that he was cold and stiff. And he felt them himself, and said: When the poison reaches the heart, that will be the end.

He was beginning to grow cold about the groin, when he uncovered his face, for he had covered himself up, and said (they were his last words)-he said: Crito, I owe a cock to Asclepius; will you remember to pay the debt? The debt shall be paid, said Crito; is there anything else? There was no answer to this question; but in a minute or two a movement was heard, and the attendants uncovered him; his eyes were set, and Crito closed his eyes and mouth.

Such was the end, Echecrates, of our friend, whom I may truly call the wisest, and justest, and best of all the men whom I have ever known.

The Chapter Of Repentance Or Immunity from the *QUR'ÂN*

[5] But when the sacred months are passed away, kill the idolaters wherever ye may find them; and take them, and besiege them, and lie in wait for them in every place of observation; but if they repent, and are steadfast in prayer, and give alms, then let them go their way; verily, God is forgiving and merciful.

Odysseus Toetet die Freier
Source: Gustav Schwab: "Sagen des Klassischen Altertums"

Chapter Seventeen, Glory

There are multiple types of glory. Jesus asked the Father to glorify Him so that He may glorify the Father. Another glory, the reflection of God, is seen in the universe. A lesser glory is in the fanfare that a man can surround himself with in his life. Pretense is pretend and flaunting is fake. Humans are tainted creatures; we will not have our glory until we are in the Kingdom of God reflecting the glory of the Lord. We must refrain from holding ourselves up until God brings us up into Glory Land.

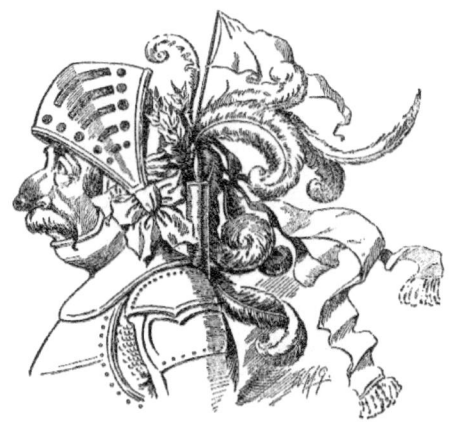

Crest of a Popular Knight

"He wore a crest on his helmet adorned with German favors given him by lady admirers, so that the crest of a popular young knight often looked like a slump at the Bon marché."

Source: Bill Nye: "Bill Nye's History of England"
Cartoonist: W. M. Goodes

~

17:1 These words spake Jesus, and lifted up his eyes to heaven, and said, Father, the hour is come; glorify thy Son, that thy Son also may glorify thee: 17:2 As thou hast given him power over all flesh, that he should give eternal life to as many as thou hast given him.
17:3 And this is life eternal, that they might know thee the only true

God, and Jesus Christ, whom thou hast sent.

17:4 I have glorified thee on the earth: I have finished the work which thou gavest me to do. 17:5 And now, O Father, glorify thou me with thine own self with the glory which I had with thee before the world was. 17:6 I have manifested thy name unto the men which thou gavest me out of the world: thine they were, and thou gavest them me; and they have kept thy word. 17:7 Now they have known that all things whatsoever thou hast given me are of thee. 17:8 For I have given unto them the words which thou gavest me; and they have received them, and have known surely that I came out from thee, and they have believed that thou didst send me. 17:9 I pray for them: I pray not for the world, but for them which thou hast given me; for they are thine.

17:10 And all mine are thine, and thine are mine; and I am glorified in them. 17:11 And now I am no more in the world, but these are in the world, and I come to thee. Holy Father, keep through thine own name those whom thou hast given me, that they may be one, as we are.

17:12 While I was with them in the world, I kept them in thy name: those that thou gavest me I have kept, and none of them is lost, but the son of perdition; that the scripture might be fulfilled.

17:13 And now come I to thee; and these things I speak in the world, that they might have my joy fulfilled in themselves. 17:14 I have given them thy word; and the world hath hated them, because they are not of the world, even as I am not of the world. 17:15 I pray not that thou shouldest take them out of the world, but that thou shouldest keep them from the evil.

17:16 They are not of the world, even as I am not of the world.

17:17 Sanctify them through thy truth: thy word is truth.

17:18 As thou hast sent me into the world, even so have I also sent them into the world. 17:19 And for their sakes I sanctify myself, that they also might be sanctified through the truth.

17:20 Neither pray I for these alone, but for them also which shall believe on me through their word; 17:21 That they all may be one; as thou, Father, art in me, and I in thee, that they also may be one in us: that the world may believe that thou hast sent me.

17:22 And the glory which thou gavest me I have given them; that they may be one, even as we are one: 17:23 I in them, and thou in me, that they may be made perfect in one; and that the world may know that thou hast sent me, and hast loved them, as thou hast loved me.

17:24 Father, I will that they also, whom thou hast given me, be with me where I am; that they may behold my glory, which thou hast given me: for thou lovedst me before the foundation of the world.

17:25 O righteous Father, the world hath not known thee: but I have known thee, and these have known that thou hast sent me.

17:26 And I have declared unto them thy name, and will declare it: that the love wherewith thou hast loved me may be in them, and I in them.

What is the central theme of Jesus' prayer? Why?

_____
_____
_____
_____
_____
_____
_____

The Haunter of the Dark
by H.P. Lovecraft

I have seen the dark universe yawning
Where the black planets roll without aim,
Where they roll in their horror unheeded,
Without knowledge or lustre or name.

Cautious investigators will hesitate to challenge the common belief that Robert Blake was killed by lightning, or by some profound nervous shock derived from an electrical discharge. It is true that the window he faced was unbroken, but nature has shown herself capable of many freakish performances.

The Twelve Signs of the Zodiac
Source: Ebenezer Sibly: "Astrology"

172

Chapter Eighteen, Vices & Virtues

In this world there are a cornucopia of vices and virtues; the amount of each that a woman has is up to her to decide. Whether one follows the path of a monk or the path of pagan worship of Astaroth, God looks at the heart; the purposes behind our actions are apparent to God. If we give to the poor to make ourselves look good, that is all the reward we will get. If we help a stranger in need in secret, our reward will be in heaven. Our daily actions become habits of vice or virtue; choose today to increase your charity and decrease your selfishness.

Ornament: Cornucopia
Source: Francis Grose: "The Antiquities of England and Wales"

~

18:1 When Jesus had spoken these words, he went forth with his disciples over the brook Cedron, where was a garden, into the which he entered, and his disciples. 18:2 And Judas also, which betrayed him, knew the place: for Jesus ofttimes resorted thither with his disciples. 18:3 Judas then, having received a band of men and officers from the chief priests and Pharisees, cometh thither with lanterns and torches and weapons. 18:4 Jesus therefore, knowing all things that should come upon him, went forth, and said unto them, Whom seek ye?
18:5 They answered him, Jesus of Nazareth. Jesus saith unto them, I am he. And Judas also, which betrayed him, stood with them.
18:6 As soon then as he had said unto them, I am he, they went backward, and fell to the ground. 18:7 Then asked he them again,

Whom seek ye? And they said, Jesus of Nazareth.

18:8 Jesus answered, I have told you that I am he: if therefore ye seek me, let these go their way:

18:9 That the saying might be fulfilled, which he spake, Of them which thou gavest me have I lost none. 18:10 Then Simon Peter having a sword drew it, and smote the high priest's servant, and cut off his right ear. The servant's name was Malchus.

18:11 Then said Jesus unto Peter, Put up thy sword into the sheath: the cup which my Father hath given me, shall I not drink it?

18:12 Then the band and the captain and officers of the Jews took Jesus, and bound him, 18:13 And led him away to Annas first; for he was father in law to Caiaphas, which was the high priest that same year. 18:14 Now Caiaphas was he, which gave counsel to the Jews, that it was expedient that one man should die for the people.

18:15 And Simon Peter followed Jesus, and so did another disciple: that disciple was known unto the high priest, and went in with Jesus into the palace of the high priest. 18:16 But Peter stood at the door without. Then went out that other disciple, which was known unto the high priest, and spake unto her that kept the door, and brought in Peter.

18:17 Then saith the damsel that kept the door unto Peter, Art not thou also one of this man's disciples? He saith, I am not.

18:18 And the servants and officers stood there, who had made a fire of coals; for it was cold: and they warmed themselves: and Peter stood with them, and warmed himself. 18:19 The high priest then asked Jesus of his disciples, and of his doctrine. 18:20 Jesus answered him, I spake openly to the world; I ever taught in the synagogue, and in the temple, whither the Jews always resort; and in secret have I said nothing.

18:21 Why askest thou me? ask them which heard me, what I have said unto them: behold, they know what I said.

18:22 And when he had thus spoken, one of the officers which stood by struck Jesus with the palm of his hand, saying, Answerest thou the high priest so? 18:23 Jesus answered him, If I have spoken evil, bear witness of the evil: but if well, why smitest thou me? 18:24 Now Annas had sent him bound unto Caiaphas the high priest. 18:25 And Simon Peter stood and warmed himself. They said therefore unto him, Art not thou also one of his disciples? He denied it, and said, I am not.

18:26 One of the servants of the high priest, being his kinsman whose ear Peter cut off, saith, Did not I see thee in the garden with him?

18:27 Peter then denied again: and immediately the cock crew.

18:28 Then led they Jesus from Caiaphas unto the hall of judgment: and it was early; and they themselves went not into the judgment hall, lest they should be defiled; but that they might eat the passover.

18:29 Pilate then went out unto them, and said, What accusation bring ye against this man? 18:30 They answered and said unto him, If he were not a malefactor, we would not have delivered him up unto thee.

18:31 Then said Pilate unto them, Take ye him, and judge him according to your law. The Jews therefore said unto him, It is not lawful for us to put any man to death: 18:32 That the saying of Jesus might be fulfilled, which he spake, signifying what death he should die.

18:33 Then Pilate entered into the judgment hall again, and called Jesus, and said unto him, Art thou the King of the Jews?

18:34 Jesus answered him, Sayest thou this thing of thyself, or did others tell it thee of me? 18:35 Pilate answered, Am I a Jew? Thine own nation and the chief priests have delivered thee unto me: what hast thou done? 18:36 Jesus answered, My kingdom is not of this world: if my kingdom were of this world, then would my servants fight, that I should not be delivered to the Jews: but now is my kingdom not from hence.

18:37 Pilate therefore said unto him, Art thou a king then? Jesus answered, Thou sayest that I am a king. To this end was I born, and for this cause came I into the world, that I should bear witness unto the truth. Every one that is of the truth heareth my voice.

18:38 Pilate saith unto him, What is truth? And when he had said this, he went out again unto the Jews, and saith unto them, I find in him no fault at all. 18:39 But ye have a custom, that I should release unto you one at the passover: will ye therefore that I release unto you the King of the Jews? 18:40 Then cried they all again, saying, Not this man, but Barabbas. Now Barabbas was a robber.

What caused the crowd to fall backward to the ground?

_____
_____
_____
_____
_____
_____
_____

Ten Virtues Of Monks
Complied by Pravin K. Shah

Along with the five great vows, monks strive after the tenfold virtues of a self controlled ascetic. The layperson follows these virtues partially.

Kshamaa...Forbearance, Forgiveness
Maardava...Modesty, Humility
Aarjava..Straightforwardness, Candor
Saucha..Contentment
Satya..Truthfullness
Samyam...Self-restraint, Control of Senses
Tapa..Austerity, Penance
Tyaga...Renunciation
Akinchanya...Non-attachment
Brahmacharya..Celibacy, Chastity

Seal of Astaroth.

He is a Mighty, Strong Duke, and appeareth in the Form of an hurtful Angel riding on an Infernal Beast like a Dragon, and carrying in his right hand a Viper. Thou must in no wise let him approach too near unto thee, lest he do thee damage by his Noisome Breath.

Source: Samuel MacGregor Liddel Mathers: "The Goetia: The Lesser Key of Solomon the King"

Chapter Nineteen, Reality & Fantasy

Many people disagree over what is real and what is fake. Some people believe that the Garden of Eden story is literal, and that there was a historical Jesus, while others think the Biblical creation story is a myth and that Jesus never lived. And yet, most people agree that Shakespeare was real, while regarding his character Queen Mab as a fantasy. Human reason and faith must dictate over emotion and imagination to tell what is real. Base your beliefs on reality; weigh the evidence carefully. Do not let moods or daydreams determine veracity.

The Serpent & Eve.
Source: Francis Quarles: "Emblems Divine and Moral"

~

19:1 Then Pilate therefore took Jesus, and scourged him.
19:2 And the soldiers platted a crown of thorns, and put it on his head, and they put on him a purple robe, 19:3 And said, Hail, King of the Jews! and they smote him with their hands.
19:4 Pilate therefore went forth again, and saith unto them, Behold, I bring him forth to you, that ye may know that I find no fault in him.
19:5 Then came Jesus forth, wearing the crown of thorns, and the purple robe. And Pilate saith unto them, Behold the man!

19:6 When the chief priests therefore and officers saw him, they cried out, saying, Crucify him, crucify him. Pilate saith unto them, Take ye him, and crucify him: for I find no fault in him.

19:7 The Jews answered him, We have a law, and by our law he ought to die, because he made himself the Son of God.

19:8 When Pilate therefore heard that saying, he was the more afraid; 19:9 And went again into the judgment hall, and saith unto Jesus, Whence art thou? But Jesus gave him no answer.

19:10 Then saith Pilate unto him, Speakest thou not unto me? knowest thou not that I have power to crucify thee, and have power to release thee? 19:11 Jesus answered, Thou couldest have no power at all against me, except it were given thee from above: therefore he that delivered me unto thee hath the greater sin. 19:12 And from thenceforth Pilate sought to release him: but the Jews cried out, saying, If thou let this man go, thou art not Caesar's friend: whosoever maketh himself a king speaketh against Caesar. 19:13 When Pilate therefore heard that saying, he brought Jesus forth, and sat down in the judgment seat in a place that is called the Pavement, but in the Hebrew, Gabbatha. 19:14 And it was the preparation of the passover, and about the sixth hour: and he saith unto the Jews, Behold your King! 19:15 But they cried out, Away with him, away with him, crucify him. Pilate saith unto them, Shall I crucify your King? The chief priests answered, We have no king but Caesar. 19:16 Then delivered he him therefore unto them to be crucified. And they took Jesus, and led him away. 19:17 And he bearing his cross went forth into a place called the place of a skull, which is called in the Hebrew Golgotha: 19:18 Where they crucified him, and two others with him, on either side one, and Jesus in the midst.

19:19 And Pilate wrote a title, and put it on the cross. And the writing was, JESUS OF NAZARETH THE KING OF THE JEWS.

19:20 This title then read many of the Jews: for the place where Jesus was crucified was nigh to the city: and it was written in Hebrew, and Greek, and Latin. 19:21 Then said the chief priests of the Jews to Pilate, Write not, The King of the Jews; but that he said, I am King of the Jews. 19:22 Pilate answered, What I have written I have written.

19:23 Then the soldiers, when they had crucified Jesus, took his garments, and made four parts, to every soldier a part; and also his coat: now the coat was without seam, woven from the top throughout.

19:24 They said therefore among themselves, Let us not rend it, but cast lots for it, whose it shall be: that the scripture might be fulfilled, which saith, They parted my raiment among them, and for my vesture they did cast lots. These things therefore the soldiers did.

19:25 Now there stood by the cross of Jesus his mother, and his mother's sister, Mary the wife of Cleophas, and Mary Magdalene.

19:26 When Jesus therefore saw his mother, and the disciple standing by, whom he loved, he saith unto his mother, Woman, behold thy son! 19:27 Then saith he to the disciple, Behold thy mother! And from that hour that disciple took her unto his own home. 19:28 After this, Jesus knowing that all things were now accomplished, that the scripture might be fulfilled, saith, I thirst. 19:29 Now there was set a vessel full of vinegar: and they filled a spunge with vinegar, and put it upon hyssop, and put it to his mouth. 19:30 When Jesus therefore had received the vinegar, he said, It is finished: and he bowed his head, and gave up the ghost. 19:31 The Jews therefore, because it was the preparation, that the bodies should not remain upon the cross on the sabbath day, (for that sabbath day was an high day,) besought Pilate that their legs might be broken, and that they might be taken away.

19:32 Then came the soldiers, and brake the legs of the first, and of the other which was crucified with him. 19:33 But when they came to Jesus, and saw that he was dead already, they brake not his legs:

19:34 But one of the soldiers with a spear pierced his side, and forthwith came there out blood and water.

19:35 And he that saw it bare record, and his record is true: and he knoweth that he saith true, that ye might believe.

19:36 For these things were done, that the scripture should be fulfilled, A bone of him shall not be broken.

19:37 And again another scripture saith, They shall look on him whom they pierced. 19:38 And after this Joseph of Arimathaea, being a disciple of Jesus, but secretly for fear of the Jews, besought Pilate that he might take away the body of Jesus: and Pilate gave him leave. He came therefore, and took the body of Jesus. 19:39 And there came also Nicodemus, which at the first came to Jesus by night, and brought a mixture of myrrh and aloes, about an hundred pound weight.

19:40 Then took they the body of Jesus, and wound it in linen clothes with the spices, as the manner of the Jews is to bury. 19:41 Now in the place where he was crucified there was a garden; and in the garden a new sepulchre, wherein was never man yet laid. 19:42 There laid they Jesus therefore because of the Jews' preparation day; for the sepulchre was nigh at hand.

How do the chapter pictures and the chapter text relate?

_____
_____
_____
_____
_____
_____
_____

Chapter Three from *The Proslogion*
by Saint Anselm

So truly, therefore, dost thou exist, O Lord, my God, that thou canst not be conceived not to exist; and rightly. For, if a mind could conceive of a being better than thee, the creature would rise above the Creator; and this is most absurd. And, indeed, whatever else there is, except thee alone, can be conceived not to exist. To thee alone, therefore, it belongs to exist more truly than all other beings, and hence in a higher degree than all others. For, whatever else exists does not exist so truly, and hence in a less degree it belongs to it to exist. Why, then, has the fool said in his heart, there is no God (Psalms 14:1), since it is so evident, to a rational mind, that thou dost exist in the highest degree of all? Why, except that he is dull and a fool?

Queen Mab is a fairy with butterfly wings who brings dreams to people.
She was described by Shakespeare in Romeo and Juliet.

Source: Edgar, M. G.: "A Treasury of Verse for Little Children" (1923)

Artist: Willy Pogany (– 1955)

Chapter Twenty, Life

The chasm between death and life was forever bridged by the death of Jesus. No longer will men have to be trapped on the side of death; believers can now move from mortal life to life eternal by sharing in the life of Christ.

The King's Crown
Source: Nicholas Caussin: "The Holy Court" (1663)

~

20:1 The first day of the week cometh Mary Magdalene early, when it was yet dark, unto the sepulchre, and seeth the stone taken away from the sepulchre. 20:2 Then she runneth, and cometh to Simon Peter, and to the other disciple, whom Jesus loved, and saith unto them, They have taken away the Lord out of the sepulchre, and we know not where they have laid him.

20:3 Peter therefore went forth, and that other disciple, and came to the sepulchre. 20:4 So they ran both together: and the other disciple did outrun Peter, and came first to the sepulchre.

20:5 And he stooping down, and looking in, saw the linen clothes lying; yet went he not in. 20:6 Then cometh Simon Peter following him, and went into the sepulchre, and seeth the linen clothes lie,

20:7 And the napkin, that was about his head, not lying with the linen clothes, but wrapped together in a place by itself. 20:8 Then went in also that other disciple, which came first to the sepulchre, and he saw, and believed. 20:9 For as yet they knew not the scripture, that he must rise again from the dead. 20:10 Then the disciples went away again unto their own home. 20:11 But Mary stood without at the sepulchre weeping: and as she wept, she stooped down, and looked into the sepulchre,

20:12 And seeth two angels in white sitting, the one at the head, and the other at the feet, where the body of Jesus had lain.

20:13 And they say unto her, Woman, why weepest thou? She saith unto them, Because they have taken away my Lord, and I know not where they have laid him. 20:14 And when she had thus said, she turned herself back, and saw Jesus standing, and knew not that it was Jesus. 20:15 Jesus saith unto her, Woman, why weepest thou? Whom seekest thou? She, supposing him to be the gardener, saith unto him, Sir, if thou have borne him hence, tell me where thou hast laid him, and I will take him away. 20:16 Jesus saith unto her, Mary. She turned herself, and saith unto him, Rabboni; which is to say, Master. 20:17 Jesus saith unto her, Touch me not; for I am not yet ascended to my Father: but go to my brethren, and say unto them, I ascend unto my Father, and your Father; and to my God, and your God. 20:18 Mary Magdalene came and told the disciples that she had seen the Lord, and that he had spoken these things unto her.

20:19 Then the same day at evening, being the first day of the week, when the doors were shut where the disciples were assembled for fear of the Jews, came Jesus and stood in the midst, and saith unto them, Peace be unto you. 20:20 And when he had so said, he shewed unto them his hands and his side. Then were the disciples glad, when they saw the Lord. 20:21 Then said Jesus to them again, Peace be unto you: as my Father hath sent me, even so send I you. 20:22 And when he had said this, he breathed on them, and saith unto them, Receive ye the Holy Ghost: 20:23 Whose soever sins ye remit, they are remitted unto them; and whose soever sins ye retain, they are retained.

20:24 But Thomas, one of the twelve, called Didymus, was not with them when Jesus came. 20:25 The other disciples therefore said unto him, We have seen the Lord. But he said unto them, Except I shall see in his hands the print of the nails, and put my finger into the print of the nails, and thrust my hand into his side, I will not believe.

20:26 And after eight days again his disciples were within, and Thomas with them: then came Jesus, the doors being shut, and stood in the midst, and said, Peace be unto you. 20:27 Then saith he to Thomas, reach hither thy finger, and behold my hands; and reach hither thy hand,

and thrust it into my side: and be not faithless, but believing.

20:28 And Thomas answered and said unto him, My Lord and my God.

20:29 Jesus saith unto him, Thomas, because thou hast seen me, thou hast believed: blessed are they that have not seen, and yet have believed. 20:30 And many other signs truly did Jesus in the presence of his disciples, which are not written in this book:

20:31 But these are written, that ye might believe that Jesus is the Christ, the Son of God; and that believing ye might have life through his name.

Do you ever act like Doubting Thomas?

_____

_____

_____

_____

_____

_____

_____

Act Three, Scene One from *Hamlet* by William Shakespeare

HAMLET:
To be, or not to be: that is the question:
Whether 'tis nobler in the mind to suffer
The slings and arrows of outrageous fortune,
Or to take arms against a sea of troubles,
And by opposing end them? To die: to sleep;
No more; and by a sleep to say we end
The heart-ache and the thousand natural shocks
That flesh is heir to, 'tis a consummation
Devoutly to be wish'd. To die, to sleep;
To sleep: perchance to dream: ay, there's the rub;
For in that sleep of death what dreams may come
When we have shuffled off this mortal coil,
Must give us pause: there's the respect
That makes calamity of so long life;

183

For who would bear the whips and scorns of time,
The oppressor's wrong, the proud man's contumely,
The pangs of despised love, the law's delay,
The insolence of office and the spurns
That patient merit of the unworthy takes,
When he himself might his quietus make
With a bare bodkin? who would fardels bear,
To grunt and sweat under a weary life,
But that the dread of something after death,
The undiscover'd country from whose bourn
No traveller returns, puzzles the will
And makes us rather bear those ills we have
Than fly to others that we know not of?
Thus conscience does make cowards of us all;
And thus the native hue of resolution
Is sicklied o'er with the pale cast of thought,
And enterprises of great pitch and moment
With this regard their currents turn awry,
And lose the name of action.

Ophelia is perhaps Hamlet's former lover. She sits by the river plucking
flowers one by one and worrying them in her hands; shortly afterwards
she drowns herself.

Source: William Shakespeare: "The Works of Shakspere, with notes by
Charles Knight"

Artist: A. Hughes
Engraver: C. Cousin

Chapter Twenty-One, Lamb & Lion

At his first coming, Jesus appeared as a meek and humble lamb; at his second coming, he shall broach the heavens as the King of kings and the Lion of Judah. Forgiveness was brought, now judgment remains to be received. Have you received forgiveness or are you waiting for judgment?

Two Cherubs
Source: John Ray: "A Compleat Collection of English Proverbs"

~

21:1 After these things Jesus shewed himself again to the disciples at the sea of Tiberias; and on this wise shewed he himself.
21:2 There were together Simon Peter, and Thomas called Didymus, and Nathanael of Cana in Galilee, and the sons of Zebedee, and two other of his disciples. 21:3 Simon Peter saith unto them, I go a fishing. They say unto him, We also go with thee. They went forth, and entered into a ship immediately; and that night they caught nothing.
21:4 But when the morning was now come, Jesus stood on the shore: but the disciples knew not that it was Jesus. 21:5 Then Jesus saith unto them, Children, have ye any meat? They answered him, No.
21:6 And he said unto them, Cast the net on the right side of the ship, and ye shall find. They cast therefore, and now they were not able to draw it for the multitude of fishes. 21:7 Therefore that disciple whom Jesus loved saith unto Peter, It is the Lord. Now when Simon Peter

heard that it was the Lord, he girt his fisher's coat unto him, (for he was naked,) and did cast himself into the sea. 21:8 And the other disciples came in a little ship; (for they were not far from land, but as it were two hundred cubits,) dragging the net with fishes. 21:9 As soon then as they were come to land, they saw a fire of coals there, and fish laid thereon, and bread.

21:10 Jesus saith unto them, Bring of the fish which ye have now caught. 21:11 Simon Peter went up, and drew the net to land full of great fishes, and hundred and fifty and three: and for all there were so many, yet was not the net broken. 21:12 Jesus saith unto them, Come and dine. And none of the disciples durst ask him, Who art thou? knowing that it was the Lord.

21:13 Jesus then cometh, and taketh bread, and giveth them, and fish likewise. 21:14 This is now the third time that Jesus shewed himself to his disciples, after that he was risen from the dead. 21:15 So when they had dined, Jesus saith to Simon Peter, Simon, son of Jonas, lovest thou me more than these? He saith unto him, Yea, Lord; thou knowest that I love thee. He saith unto him, Feed my lambs. 21:16 He saith to him again the second time, Simon, son of Jonas, lovest thou me? He saith unto him, Yea, Lord; thou knowest that I love thee. He saith unto him, Feed my sheep. 21:17 He saith unto him the third time, Simon, son of Jonas lovest thou me? Peter was grieved because he said unto him the third time, Lovest thou me? And he said unto him, Lord, thou knowest all things; thou knowest that I love thee. Jesus saith unto him, Feed my sheep. 21:18 Verily, verily, I say unto thee, When thou wast young, thou girdedst thyself, and walkedst whither thou wouldest: but when thou shalt be old, thou shalt stretch forth thy hands, and another shall gird thee, and carry thee whither thou wouldest not. 21:19 This spake he, signifying by what death he should glorify God. And when he had spoken this, he saith unto him, Follow me. 21:20 Then Peter, turning about, seeth the disciple whom Jesus loved following; which also leaned on his breast at supper, and said, Lord, which is he that betrayeth thee? 21:21 Peter seeing him saith to Jesus, Lord, and what shall this man do? 21:22 Jesus saith unto him, If I will that he tarry till I come, what is that to thee? follow thou me. 21:23 Then went this saying abroad among the brethren, that that disciple should not die: yet Jesus said not unto him, He shall not die; but, If I will that he tarry till I come, what is that to thee? 21:24 This is the disciple which testifieth of these things, and wrote these things: and we know that his testimony is true.

21:25 And there are also many other things which Jesus did, the which, if they should be written every one, I suppose that even the world itself could not contain the books that should be written. Amen.

What do you think are some of the actions that Jesus performed that are not recorded in the Gospel of John?

_____
_____
_____
_____
_____
_____
_____
_____

The Lamb by William Blake

LITTLE lamb, who made thee?
Dost thou know who made thee,
Gave thee life, and bade thee feed
By the stream and o'er the mead;
Gave thee clothing of delight,
Softest clothing, woolly, bright;
Gave thee such a tender voice,
Making all the vales rejoice?
Little lamb, who made thee?
Dost thou know who made thee?
Little lamb, I'll tell thee;
Little lamb, I'll tell thee;
He is called by thy name,
For He calls Himself a lamb;
He is meek and He is mild,
He became a little child.
I a child and thou a lamb,
We are called by His name.
Little lamb, God bless thee!
Little lamb, God bless thee!

There are two choices for an eternal abode.

Heaven or Hell?

The Book of Revelation

20:1 And I saw an angel come down from **heaven**, having the key of the **bottomless pit** and a great chain in his hand.

20:2 And he laid hold on the dragon, that old serpent, which is the Devil, and Satan, and bound him a thousand years,
20:3 And cast him into the **bottomless pit**, and shut him up, and set a seal upon him, that he should deceive the nations no more, till the thousand years should be fulfilled: and after that he must be loosed a little season. 20:4 And I saw thrones, and they sat upon them, and judgment was given unto them: and I saw the souls of them that were beheaded for the witness of Jesus, and for the word of **God**, and which had not **worshiped** the **beast**, neither his image, neither had received his mark upon their foreheads, or in their hands; and they lived and reigned with Christ a thousand years. 20:5 But the rest of the dead lived not again until the thousand years were finished. This is the first resurrection. 20:6 *Blessed* and holy is he that hath part in the first resurrection: on such the second death hath no power, but they shall be priests of God and of ***Christ***, and shall reign with him a thousand years. 20:7 And when the thousand years are expired, Satan shall be loosed out of his prison, 20:8 And shall go out to deceive the nations which are in the four quarters of the earth, Gog and Magog, to gather them together to battle: the number of whom is as the sand of the sea. 20:9 And they went up on the breadth of the earth, and compassed the camp of the saints about, and the beloved city: and fire came down from God out of heaven, and devoured them.

20:10 And the devil that deceived them was cast into the lake of fire and brimstone, where the beast and the false prophet are, and shall be tormented day and night for ever and ever. 20:11 And I saw a great white throne, and him that sat on it, from whose face the

earth and the heaven fled away; and there was found no place for them. 20:12 And I saw the dead, small and great, stand before God; and the **books** were opened: and another book was opened, which is the book of life: and the dead were judged out of those things which were written in the books, according to their works. 20:13 And the sea gave up the dead which were in it; and death and hell delivered up the dead which were in them: and they were judged every man according to their works. 20:14 And **death and hell** were cast into the *lake of fire*. This is the second death.

20:15 And whosoever was not found written in the book of life was cast into the *lake of fire*.

21:1 And I saw a new heaven and a new earth: for the first heaven and the first earth were passed away; and there was no more sea.

21:2 And I **John** saw the holy city, new Jerusalem, coming down from God out of heaven, prepared as a bride adorned for her husband.

21:3 And I heard a great voice out of heaven saying, Behold, the tabernacle of God is with men, and he will dwell with them, and they shall be his people, and God himself shall be with them, and be their

God. 21:4 And God shall **wipe away all tears** from their eyes; and there shall be no more death, neither sorrow, nor crying,

neither shall there be any more **pain**: for the former things are passed

away. 21:5 And he that sat upon the throne said, **Behold**, I make all things new. And he said unto me, Write: for these words are true and faithful. 21:6 And he said unto me, It is done. I am Alpha and Omega, the beginning and the end. I will give unto him that is

athirst of the fountain of the water of life freely.

21:7 He that overcometh shall inherit all things; and I will be his God, and he shall be my son. 21:8 But the fearful, and unbelieving, and the abominable, and murderers, and **whoremongers**, and sorcerers, and idolaters, and all liars, shall have their part in the lake which burneth with fire and brimstone: which is the second death.

21:9 And there came unto me one of the seven angels which had the seven vials full of the seven last plagues, and talked with me, saying, Come hither, I will shew thee the bride, the **Lamb's wife**.

21:10 And he carried me away in the spirit to a great and high mountain, and shewed me that great city, the holy Jerusalem, descending out of heaven from God, 21:11 Having the glory of God: and her light was like unto a stone most ***precious***, even like a jasper stone, clear as crystal; 21:12 And had a wall great and high, and had twelve gates, and at the gates twelve angels, and names written thereon, which are the names of the twelve tribes of the children of Israel:

21:13 On the east three gates; on the north three gates; on the south three gates; and on the west three gates. 21:14 And the wall of the city had twelve foundations, and in them the names of the twelve apostles of the Lamb. 21:15 And he that talked with me had a golden reed to measure the city, and the gates thereof, and the wall thereof.

21:16 And the city lieth foursquare, and the length is as large as the breadth: and he measured the city with the reed, twelve thousand furlongs. The length and the breadth and the height of it are equal.

21:17 And he measured the wall thereof, an hundred and forty and four cubits, according to the measure of a man, that is, of the angel.

21:18 And the building of the wall of it was of jasper: and the city was pure gold, like unto clear glass.

21:19 And the foundations of the wall of the city were garnished with all manner of precious *stones*. The first foundation was jasper; the second, sapphire; the third, a chalcedony; the fourth, an emerald; 21:20 The fifth, sardonyx; the sixth, sardius; the seventh, chrysolite; the eighth, beryl; the ninth, a topaz; the tenth, a chrysoprasus; the eleventh, a jacinth; the twelfth, an amethyst. 21:21 And the twelve gates were twelve pearls; every several gate was of *one pearl*: and the street of the city was pure gold, as it were transparent glass. 21:22 And I saw no temple therein: for the Lord God Almighty and the Lamb are the temple of it.

21:23 And the city had no need of the **SUN**, neither of the **moon**, to shine in it: for the glory of God did lighten it, and the Lamb is the light thereof. 21:24 And the nations of them which are saved shall walk in the light of it: and the kings of the earth do bring their glory and honour into it. 21:25 And the gates of it shall not be shut at all by day: for there shall be no night there.

21:26 And they shall bring the **glory and honour** of the nations into it. 21:27 And there shall in no wise enter into it any thing that defileth, neither whatsoever worketh abomination, or maketh a lie: but they which are written in the **Lamb's book of life**.
22:1 And he shewed me a pure river of water of life, clear as crystal,

proceeding out of the throne of God and of the Lamb.

22:2 In the midst of the street of it, and on either side of **the river**, was there the tree of life, which bare twelve manner of fruits, and

yielded her fruit every month: and the leaves of the *tree* were for the

healing of the nations. 22:3 And there shall be no more curse: but the throne of God and of the Lamb shall be in it; and his servants shall serve him:

22:4 And they shall see his face; and his name shall be in their foreheads. 22:5 And there shall be no night there; and they need no candle, neither light of the sun; for the Lord God giveth them light: and they shall reign for ever and ever. 22:6 And he said unto me, These

sayings are faithful and true: and the Lord God of the holy prophets sent his angel to shew unto his servants the things which must shortly be done.
22:7 Behold, I come quickly: blessed is he that keepeth the sayings of the prophecy of this book. 22:8 And I John saw these things, and heard

them. And when I had heard and seen, I fell down to worship

before the feet of the angel which shewed me these things.

22:9 Then saith he unto me, See thou do it not: for I am thy fellowservant, and of thy brethren the prophets, and of them which keep the sayings of this book: **worship God**.

22:10 And he saith unto me, Seal not the sayings of the prophecy of this book: for the time is at hand. 22:11 He that is unjust, let him be unjust still: and he which is filthy, let him be filthy still: and he that is righteous, let him be righteous still: and he that is holy, let him be holy still. 22:12 And, behold, I come quickly; and my reward is with me, to give every man according as his work shall be.

22:13 I am **Alpha and Omega**, the beginning and the end, the first and the last.

22:14 Blessed are they that do his commandments, that they may have right to the tree of life, and may enter in through the gates into the city.

22:15 For without are dogs, and sorcerers, and whoremongers, and murderers, and idolaters, and whosoever loveth and maketh a *lie*.

22:16 I Jesus have sent mine angel to testify unto you these things in the churches. I am the root and the offspring of David, and the bright and morning star. 22:17 And the Spirit and the bride say, Come. And let him that heareth say, Come. And let him that is athirst come. And whosoever will, let him take the water of life freely.

22:18 For I testify unto every man that heareth the words of the prophecy of this book, If any man shall add unto these things, God shall add unto him the plagues that are written in this book: 22:19 And if any man shall take away from the words of the book of this prophecy, God shall take away his part out of the book of life, and out of the holy city, and from the things which are written in this book.

22:20 He which testifieth these things saith, Surely I come quickly. Amen. Even so, come, *Lord Jesus*.

22:21 The grace of our Lord Jesus Christ be with you all. Amen.

Please visit NewLifeFromHeaven.com.

This site is for Christians, those looking for God, and those running from God!

Mission:

To reach all souls with the saving power of Christ's love thus bringing them new life from heaven.

Objectives:

*To spread the simple way of salvation by means of the overall website and specifically by "The Gospel" Page!

*To increase exposure to other Christian websites!

*To carry out the goals of the "Donation Page!"

Thank You Sacred-Texts.com!

Your collection of public domain texts has filled The Void!

The following is a grateful advertisement:

Buy Sacred-texts on Disk

"Own a complete library of
the most influential books of all time!"

eastern religions. Get English translations of all of the Vedas, together for the first time. Read the beloved Hindu epics, the Mahabharata and Ramayana. Included are many volumes of the renowned Sacred Books of the East series, including the Upanishads, the Bhagavad Gita, Taoist Texts, the Dhammapada, the Lotus Sutra, I Ching and the Confucian Canon. You can also read the historical sources of Wicca, New Age beliefs, and even Atheism. Whatever your religious beliefs, this is a must-have if you want to understand world religions. No other religious studies disk is as comprehensive or well-organized.

You get hundreds of books about oral traditions and folklore that go back to the dawn of humanity. Take a trip to the Kalahari, Siberia, or the Australian outback and hear the oldest stories in the world from tribal elders and shamans. Sail with the ancient Polynesians from New Zealand to Hawaii and Easter Island. Follow the adventures of tricksters, culture heroes and animals from Native America. Journey back to ancient Rome and Greece and feast on rich classical mythology. Enjoy the legends and sagas of the European dark ages, and wonderful Celtic folklore of gods, heroes and fairies. Read all of the primary sources of Tolkien's Lord of the Rings, including the Kalevala and the Eddas. Open up dusty--and very authentic--books of magic, peer into the future with Nostradamus, get a Tarot reading, visit legendary lost continents and learn occult secrets--if you dare. All of these and more are included on the disk.

Visit Sacred-Texts.com Now!

"I highly recommend this to both the professional clergy, and the amateur researcher. It saves the wait for Internet connections and web page loads, and provides a broad range of documents."

-Amazon customer review.

"Unbelievable. A lovingly chosen library of sacred and non-sacred texts and classics of great literature. It's huge. It would cost tens of thousands of dollars in paper form. Now, thanks to cheap scanning technology and the cd-rom format all of these books can sit comfortably on 1 CD!!!! Even 10 years ago we wouldn't have believed this possible. Highly recommended. You simply can't go wrong..."

-Amazon customer review.

Notes

www.ingramcontent.com/pod-product-compliance
Lightning Source LLC
Chambersburg PA
CBHW021600280526
45784CB00001BA/438